*The Undergraduate Curriculum
in Higher Education*

THE LIBRARY OF EDUCATION

A Project of The Center for Applied Research in Education, Inc.
G. R. Gottschalk, Director

Categories of Coverage

I	II	III
Curriculum and Teaching	Administration, Organization, and Finance	Psychology

IV	V	VI
History, Philosophy, and Social Foundations	Professional Skills	Educational Institutions

The Undergraduate Curriculum
in Higher Education

PAUL L. DRESSEL

Director, Office of Institutional Research
Michigan State University

1963
The Center for Applied Research in Education, Inc.
Washington, D.C.

LIBRARY OF CONGRESS
CATALOG CARD NO.: 63–8461

PRINTED IN THE UNITED STATES OF AMERICA
C 9000

Foreword

The purpose of this study of the undergraduate curriculum of colleges and universities is to analyze the nature of and the assumptions underlying present curriculums, and to offer suggestions for their reform.

The reader may approach the book with a high degree of confidence for the reason that the author, Dr. Paul L. Dressel, is a leading examiner of such curricula. His numerous studies of institutions and his constructive contributions to the literature on the objectives of education and on evaluations of achievement have made him a widely recognized authority on his subject. This book extends one's impression of him as an objective critic of higher education.

The subject is timely. From time to time in the history of higher education fresh directions for learning have been devised. Thus we may reflect upon the successive concepts of the trivium and quadrivium, the classics, the elective curricula, the distribution plan, general education, and others—each of which has had its period of acceptance. What over-all concept, what set of principles governs the undergraduate curriculum of today? It would not be far from correct to say that it has merely "grown up" like Topsy. The present array of courses is a result of many impacts on the colleges—arising from depression, war, and post-war conditions—which have induced innumerable expediencies and compromises.

Change is urgently needed. The pressures from the environment, the demands of students, the needs of the society, the necessity for economical operations—all of these factors suggest strongly the desirability of making substantial revisions in curriculum and program.

Dr. Dressel's monograph is rich in its suggestions for revision. Of even greater importance, he defines a set of principles to serve as guidelines in achieving the over-all purpose.

ALGO D. HENDERSON
*Director, Center for the Study
of Higher Education*
University of Michigan

Contents

The Undergraduate Curriculum
in Higher Education

CHAPTER I

Some Historical Notes
and Trends in Higher Education

The profuse course offerings which characterize the curriculums
of the vast majority of colleges and universities today bear little
similarity in titles or in organization to the limited curriculums of
the early American colleges. Existing curriculums have developed
partly out of identifiable needs in American society and partly out
of the rapid expansion of knowledge which has characterized the
past century. The patterns which have emerged in the attempt to
cope with these developments pose complex problems. These may
be better understood, though by no means resolved, by a brief historical survey of American higher education.

The curriculum of the early American college was adapted from
that of the English college. This prescribed curriculum, planned to
provide an education suitable for a community of gentlemen, assumed a more or less fixed body of knowledge which consisted of
the medieval liberal arts (not including music), the reformed
philosophy of Aristotle, and studies in classical Latin, Greek, and
Hebrew, all of which were undergirded and integrated by religious
aims. The first Harvard curriculum differed but little from this
pattern. Mathematics played a minor role; natural philosophy
included what then was considered important of the natural sciences;
and moral philosophy covered the essence of political science,
economics, psychology, logic, and ethics. Probably the greatest
change up to the beginning of the Revolutionary War was the extension of the study of mathematics.

A most significant change took place at Harvard in the last third
of the eighteenth century when the Board of Overseers became
concerned because no improvement had taken place in the educational program in some years. The duties of the tutor, which had
been attached to the college class, were now to be attached to the
subject taught; each tutor now was to teach one subject to all

1

classes. Even so, the range of subjects taught by a single tutor—mathematics, physics, geography, and astronomy—would give the modern specialist professor pause. Nevertheless, from this time on, the emphasis turned increasingly to scholarship and away from personality; the professor no longer modeled the liberal education expected of the students.

Following the Revolution, the individual states became interested in the establishment and support of colleges, and the national government occasionally aided the states in the promotion of education. The relationship of the college to the church became less intimate. Higher education was becoming less class-oriented, and it was also seen as a resource for the promotion of democracy. Yet the immediate impact on the curriculum was relatively negligible. Mathematics had become more important; chemistry and physics, in simple form, were recognized, although "laboratory" consisted of a few simple experiments performed in front of the class. Such subjects as history and political economy began to appear and, by 1820, economics had appeared at Yale. Although the modern languages were introduced in the 1830's, in many cases the teachers were not regarded as part of the college faculty; additional tuition was charged, and partial or possibly no credit was given.

Most of the early experimentation with the curriculum was effectively squelched by the impact of the Yale Report of 1828. This report, which presented a detailed defense for the classical curriculum and its underlying theory of mental discipline, concluded that a common prescribed curriculum was essential, and that any practical or professional work was completely inappropriate to the college. The impact of this report insured the continuance of the prescribed classical curriculum for almost an additional half-century.

Challenges to this classical program continued. Brubacher reports:

> Affairs had come to such a pass by the middle of the 19th century that Massachusetts withdrew financial subsidies to Harvard when a special committee of the legislature reported "The college fails to answer the just expectations of the people of the State because its organization and instruction are a quarter of a century out of date." [1]

---

[1] John S. Brubacher, *A History of the Problems of Education* (New York: McGraw-Hill Book Co., Inc., 1947), p. 478.

Sciences particularly had been notoriously neglected in the old liberal education on the grounds that these had less liberal content than the humanistic studies. The startling progress of the sciences in the nineteenth century and their significance in an expanding economy and technology made it evident that the colleges could no longer ignore them.

One of the strongest challenges was made by Francis Wayland, President of Brown University, who in 1842 attacked the superficiality and unreasonably wide scope of college learning, the passivity displayed by students, and low admission requirements. He argued that a program of reform which would expand the curriculum to add courses useful to merchants, manufacturers, farmers, and others as well as nonprofessional groups, should be instituted.

It was obvious from Wayland's criticisms that not all students would be expected to cover the additional courses or topics. A necessary counterpart, then, to enlargement of the curriculum was the establishment of an elective principle permitting choice among the new subjects.

The Introduction of the Elective System

It is difficult to say when the elective system first appeared in American higher education. As early as 1779 there was some element of election in the College of William and Mary. Although students were still expected to complete a number of required courses for the degree, the student was entitled to attend the instruction of any two of three professors. In writing to George Ticknor in 1823, Jefferson spoke of allowing the students "uncontrolled choice in the lectures they shall choose to attend" and "of letting everyone come and listen to whatever he thinks may improve the condition of his mind." [2] As a result of a proposal made by Ticknor in 1825, a slight latitude of choice was permitted to Harvard students, principally in the area of modern languages.

At the University of Virginia in 1825, the students could choose one of several completely prescribed curriculums. Numerous other institutions experimented with some modified pattern of alternatives, some of which involved "second-class" degrees, such as Bachelor

---

[2] Charles F. Thwing, *A History of Higher Education in America* (New York: Appleton-Century-Crofts, Inc., 1906), pp. 312–13.

of Science or an "English Certificate." Most institutions, however, could not support the expanded faculty needed to teach a wide range of courses. This, coupled with the impact of the Yale Report, resulted in a return to the required curriculum.

Yet the interest in and demands for additional courses and alternative programs could not be silenced. The success of Rensselaer Polytechnic Institute, founded in 1824, made it evident that if the colleges would not accede to the demand, other institutions would. By 1850, Brown University, influenced by Francis Wayland, had adopted a modified elective system, although it met with little success. In the early 1850's, the University of Michigan had set up four programs leading to a Bachelor of Science degree. These attempts to expand the curriculum to meet the needs of all classes of society were reinforced by the trends of the post-Civil War years. Industrialization, the growth of large cities, the increasing expansion of knowledge—especially in the sciences, the increasing awareness of the graduate study and specialization in the European universities, and the demand of an expanding technology for specialized skills made necessary some form of advanced education more adapted to the needs of the society.

Other factors contributed to the spread of the elective system. In 1876, approximately 50,000 students were enrolled in collegiate departments and, by 1897–98, the number had increased to approximately 100,000. Thus the expansion in American economic life was associated with an expansion in college enrollments. Almost as in the present decade, this expansion and enrollment meant more funds, more buildings, more equipment, and demands for a greater variety of courses. Since the old required curriculum had already expanded in its scope to the point of treating much of the material superficially, addition of new courses could only reinforce the necessity of permitting some choice to the students. Furthermore, the appearance of a pragmatic philosophy and the destruction of the theoretical bases of the mental discipline psychology by the new experimental approaches stimulated discussion of the nature and functions of higher education and paved the way for Harvard— this time under the leadership of Charles Eliot—to support the advance of the elective principle. Under Eliot, required subjects were abolished for seniors, juniors, and sophomores in 1872, 1879, and 1894, respectively; and by 1894, even freshmen were required to take only English and a modern language. Eliot was convinced that the elective principle worked, that the needs of students were better satisfied, and that there was no extreme specialization.

Cornell University, meanwhile, under the leadership of President Andrew Dickson White, introduced five distinct general programs: (1) an arts or classical program, involving Greek and Latin; (2) a philosophical or literary program, requiring Latin and a modern language; (3) a science program, requiring science, mathematics, and the modern languages; (4) a science and letters program, requiring modern language, literature, philosophy, and some mathematics and science, and (5) an elective program with no prescribed studies. Although the elective program disappeared shortly afterward, the existence of parallel programs—each with an increasing number of elective studies—resurrected the University of Virginia pattern whereby a college curriculum met wider needs without being completely elective.

At Johns Hopkins University, where the heavy emphasis on the graduate program demanded students with a somewhat greater degree of specialization than was possible in completely prescribed programs, President Daniel C. Gilman developed a group system in 1885. Seven curriculums or groups of courses were available for student choice, but each program was almost completely prescribed. A new provision was that any individual might eliminate a particular required course by passing an examination. All students, regardless of the group they chose, faced certain common requirements in mathematics, science, Latin, and other basic areas. In general, the freshman and sophomore years were devoted to required background courses, while the last two years emphasized advanced elective work.

The advent of the completely elective system at Harvard and the adaptation of similar systems elsewhere made the parallel programs with their separate degrees appear conservative. Even so, neither electives nor group systems appeared in many institutions until after 1900. At Yale, the bulwark of the classical program, the faculty felt forced, by 1880, to introduce new courses and fields of study and to provide some options for juniors and seniors. The Sheffield Scientific School went even further in making possible preprofessional specialization in engineering and agriculture, as well as in the several sciences. Over the next quarter of a century, Yale extended the elective idea to cover the entire junior and senior years, but introduced a major-minor system to insure that the student would not use his electives unwisely.

The Major-Minor System

Although under the elective system it was possible for students to overspecialize or to complete a four-year program without taking advanced work in any field, associated factors tended to encourage specialization. More and more students were coming to college because of interests and motivations related to later vocational and economic advantages. Professors were desirous of offering courses in their own particular field of interest. Hence students were encouraged by their advisers to concentrate on one particular field of study. Also, the colleges were enrolling somewhat older students with much better preparation so that the need for a broad preparation in college seemed less important. Although Eliot found no abuses of the elective system, other observers found evidence that the student's choice among the increasingly large number of courses available was likely to be unbalanced in some significant respect.

When A. Lawrence Lowell became President of Harvard in 1909, the pressures built up by developing antagonism to the free elective system led to a demand for some unity and coherence. Lowell's solution was to introduce a system of concentration and distribution, essentially a variant of the major-minor system, which required the student to concentrate his work to the extent of taking six full-year courses in one department or field and distributing six other courses among the remaining three principal groups of study. This latter requirement forced a sampling of the important areas of knowledge while preserving some freedom of choice within each. In the junior and senior years each student was required to select a narrower field for major concentration. Aside from the distribution and concentration requirements, considerable possibility for free election by the student remained.

Payton, reporting that the earliest use he could find of the terms "major" and "minor" was in the Johns Hopkins University *Register* for the year 1877–78, quotes from it as follows:

> The major courses must be followed in any subject which the candidate offers as one of his two chief departments of work; the minor

course must be followed in (each of) those subjects taken as subsidiary.[3]

As early as 1881, David Starr Jordan while still a professor at the University of Indiana, attempted to introduce elective subjects and an elective system organized around a major study area. Later, the major-minor plan was introduced at Stanford when Jordan went there as its first president in 1891.

Payton also points out that it was primarily in the liberal arts programs that the concern arose over the possibility of a student's either overspecializing or graduating with only beginning work in a variety of fields. Preprofessional and vocational programs have always tended to follow more nearly the parallel curriculum type of pattern, with a high percentage of required courses.

Considerable variation in the interpretation of the meaning and extent of concentration developed. Thus, according to the University of California *Register* of 1905–1906, approximately half of the time of the student during his last two years was to be devoted to advanced study in a group of related courses called the major.[4] In 1925, the Knox College catalog specified a major of at least 20 semester hours in some one department.[5] A few years later the students were required to take 42 semester hours of work in a major field under the direction of a faculty adviser. In 1905, the College of William and Mary curriculum was divided into a lower and higher division. In the lower division, the students were required to take two years of work in such subjects as English, mathematics, languages, and sciences. In the upper division, the work was largely elective, but every student had to take at least 15 semester hours in a major subject. Ten years later this was expanded to 20 semester hours. By 1925, the College of William and Mary required 65 credits in general courses out of 126 credits needed for the degree. But the student now was also required to take either two majors or one major and two minors, with a major being defined as 30 credits of work in a subject and a minor as 20 credits.[6] Clearly the trend

---

[3] Phillip W. Payton, "Origins of the Terms 'Major' and 'Minor' in American Higher Education," *History of Education Quarterly,* I, No. 2 (1961), 58.

[4] Willis Rudy, *The Evolving Liberal Arts Curriculum: A Historical Review of Basic Themes* (New York: Institute of Higher Education, Teachers College, Columbia University, 1960), p. 112.

[5] *Ibid.,* p. 70.

[6] *Ibid.,* pp. 85–86.

was toward increasing both the possibility of specialization and the actual amount of specialization required.

Influence of graduate education. The idea that higher education was responsible for research extends at least as far back as Francis Bacon, but perhaps it was fully recognized and implemented only at the beginning of the nineteenth century in the Universities of Halle and Berlin. Here the emphasis was in the direction of filling each chair with a professor whose research promised to bring fame to the university. Instruction began to emphasize the "seminary" where the efforts of advanced students in original research were supervised. The Doctor of Philosophy degree was conferred at the culmination of such study, which was crowned by the publication of an independent piece of research in the form of a dissertation. There developed the twin conceptions of *Lernfreiheit* and *Lehrfreiheit* which involved, on one hand, the students' freedom to study a subject of interest, and on the other hand, the professor's freedom to teach without restraint those ideas justified by his research or falling within his area of competency. Ticknor seems to have been influenced by some of these developments in the German university as early as 1825, for it was after a trip abroad that he made the plea for the development of an elective system at Harvard. Formal graduate study, however, was not to develop for some years in the United States. Apparently the first formal graduate work without a degree was undertaken at Yale about 1847 and the Ph.D. was granted there in 1861. The first college to establish a graduate department was Harvard, in 1872. Four years later, Johns Hopkins was founded—the first American institution to be founded as a true university with emphasis on graduate study. Clark University followed the Johns Hopkins pattern in 1889.[7]

The advent of graduate instruction and the availability of American doctorates gave rise to several interrelated factors which encouraged both election and development of undergraduate specialization. No institution with academic pretensions could long be without a number of Ph.D.'s on its faculty. Prospective candidates had to be assured they would teach specialized courses, direct graduate study, and be given the opportunity for independent research. The requirement that students cover all significant known

---

[7] William E. Drake, *The American School in Transition* (Englewood Cliffs, N. J.: Prentice-Hall, Inc., 1955), pp. 316–17.

knowledge, under the assumption that the major body of truth was known and fixed, could not long endure in this atmosphere. Research tended to develop independent disciplines requiring their own departmental organization. Each department, in turn, sought for a group of students committed to study in that discipline.

Still another factor, the import of which has perhaps not always been recognized, was involved in acceptance of the Ph.D. degree as the highest and most highly respected degree in academic circles. In contrast with the original Bachelor of Arts, which was presumed to mean an acquaintance with a well-defined and commonly accepted body of knowledge encompassing the total significant heritage of man, the Ph.D. degree represented the acme of specialization. Yet each Ph.D. was accepted as the equivalent of every other. No longer could the argument prevail that only one kind of bachelor's degree was respectable, especially if that degree was to provide sufficient background to permit graduate study.

Introduction of Professional and Technical Curriculums

The development of parallel degree programs in the first quarter of the nineteenth century antedated the attention to graduate study and research. The emphasis was on applying the accumulated knowledge in the mathematics, sciences, and social sciences to solving the problems of the expanding American society and technology. This utilitarian approach contributed to the low esteem in which these alternative programs were held. Nevertheless, graduates in agriculture, home economics, engineering, veterinary medicine, and other vocational fields were useful in the economy. More and more vocational curriculums appeared, and many of them became formalized into autonomous or semiautonomous schools or colleges within the university. By 1900, four colleges of commerce were established and, by 1925, the total had reached 183.[8] These schools of college-level business education, like some of the other developing technical and professional programs, fell into several different patterns. In some cases the training was entirely at the graduate

---

[8] Richard Hofstadter and E. DeWitt Hardy, *The Development and Scope of Higher Education in the United States* (New York: Columbia University Press, 1952), p. 90.

level, with a bachelor's degree being required for admission. Other programs comprised five-year courses at the end of which was conferred a special professional bachelor's degree. Still another pattern was that of four-year programs based upon two years of liberal education and two years of professional or technical specialization. Another possibility involved the spreading of the technical or professional programs over four years, with perhaps as much as 50 per cent of the program devoted to basic liberal arts studies.

Teacher education has come to be one of the largest units in most universities, but formal preparation for teaching was not always associated with the college, although it was assumed that any college graduate could teach. With the rapid expansion of the population and of public education, it became evident that the need for teachers would not be met by the classical college graduates. Thus arose the private and public normal schools. By 1890, 92 state-supported normal schools, offering two- and three-year courses—and, in some cases, four-year courses—had been established.[9] The quality of these institutions was notoriously poor, but, so long as the new normal colleges awarded only teaching certificates or second-rate degrees in education or pedagogy, the liberal arts colleges were relatively unconcerned. The real outcry arose when the normal colleges began to confer the Bachelor of Arts degree, even though in its origin in the medieval university it would appear to have been almost exclusively a teaching degree.[10]

The new agricultural and mechanical colleges, established after the Civil War, ultimately gave considerable impetus to the development of undergraduate professional and technical programs, although extensive and sound programs were not immediately available. The early program of the Michigan Agricultural College, for example, was heavily loaded with subjects typical of the classical curriculum of the liberal arts college—largely, no doubt, because of two factors: not enough was known about agriculture to justify a large number of courses, and some of the professors recruited had major interests in the more traditional fields. Indeed, experts in scientific agriculture had yet to be trained. When the land-grant development was related to an existing university, the development

9 *Ibid.*, pp. 95–96.
10 Brubacher, *op. cit.*, pp. 514–15.

of vocational curriculums was accelerated and, after 1910, the separate land-grant colleges achieved sufficient stature to encourage others to emulate their increasingly specialized vocational offerings.

American colleges were slow to provide professional study in law and medicine, although these fields and the ministry had long been fields for which the B.A. was considered desirable. Theological schools requiring completion of a college course for admission were organized as early as 1784, 1791, and 1795. Medical schools appeared successively in 1765 in Philadelphia, in 1767 at King's College, in 1782 at Harvard, in 1797 at Dartmouth, and in 1811 at Yale. In 1893, Johns Hopkins provided for a four-year medical course after the baccalaureate degree. Although training for law was instituted in 1779 at the College of William and Mary, a law degree was not actually conferred until 1793. Harvard instituted a law school in 1817.[11] The presence of these professional programs encouraged the elective principle so that students could select those undergraduate courses which would provide the most appropriate base for later professional study.

These developments contributed further to the proliferation of courses and subjects. As the courses and subjects increased, so did the number of departments. In the 1905 announcement of the College of Literature, Science, and Arts at the University of Michigan, metallurgy, geology, drawing, mineralogy, bacteriology, analytical and applied chemistry, political economy, industry, commerce, and sociology were listed as liberal arts subjects, even though descriptions emphasized the professional or preprofessional values of their work.[12] Departmental statements, even in such fields as English, foreign languages, and philosophy, began to point out the vocational possibilities of these majors.

With the expansion in courses and departments came an expansion in degrees. The Bachelor of Science degree first came into being as a somewhat inferior degree because the classic tradition would not permit the Bachelor of Arts to be awarded to anyone who had not followed the required classical curriculum. The inclusion of the study of modern languages led to a Bachelor of Litera-

[11] William E. Drake, *The American School in Transition* (Englewood Cliffs, N.J.: Prentice-Hall, Inc., 1955), pp. 312–16.
[12] Rudy, *op. cit.*, p. 28.

ture or Bachelor of Philosophy degree. Thwing, in 1906, reported the identification of 238 different degrees.[13]

The trend toward professionalization in educational programs posed problems which are still unresolved. Law, medicine, and theology, long accepted as professions of stature, have required for graduates of accredited programs a gradually increasing amount of liberal education. Agriculture, home economics, business, and engineering curriculums have tended to become alternatives to a liberal education. The question recurringly arises as to how many professions or technical specialities require a formal program of education at the college level. The relation of such programs to a college or university poses additional issues. Theological schools frequently exist independently of colleges and universities, whereas, for the last fifty years, medicine and law have tended to associate with a university. Teacher education has moved to closer association with the liberal arts college, but the training of teachers of music, art, vocational agriculture, home economics, industrial arts, and business are among the most rigid and heavily vocational programs to be found. It is evident that the problem of relationships between liberal education and professional and technical education must be a major concern in any study of the undergraduate curriculum.

Curriculum Development Since 1900

The upsetting of the prescribed curriculum created new problems. The attempt to restore some measure of order by systems of majors and minors and the arrangements of subjects into related groups was evident between 1910 and 1920. After World War I, the general trend still seemed to be toward advancing undergraduate specialization. Independent study and honors work for the junior and senior years received almost as much attention at that time as they have in recent years. This emphasis abetted narrow specialization in advanced work and encouraged students to aim toward the Ph.D. for careers as research specialists or college professors. Rudy, in a careful study of college catalogs, has pointed out that special preprofessional courses for medicine, law, theology, dentistry, medical technology, engineering, nursing, social welfare,

[13] Thwing, *op. cit.,* p. 429.

and public service came to be one of the established features in this period.[14] In some cases combined programs were worked out which allowed students to begin the professional program in their senior year.

There were also a number of experiments of more radical nature. The work-study program of Antioch College, the College of the University of Chicago, and the Experimental College of the University of Wisconsin represented major curricular reorganization. At Swarthmore and Dartmouth instructional methods were reorganized. Bennington and Sarah Lawrence, although dissimilar in many respects, were founded on the principles of progressive education. Black Mountain College represented an attempt to found an unconventional institution more in accord with the interests of organized labor. Minnesota initiated the General College to meet the needs of students either disinterested in a four-year program or unacceptable to the units of the university offering degree programs.

General education, although a term of much longer standing than many of its users realized, came prominently into discussions of both secondary and higher education. As applied to higher education, the term has such a wide range of meanings that it is difficult to define. Its major intent seemed to be that of redefining liberal education or—even more broadly perhaps—undergraduate education in terms of aims and content suitable to the conditions existing in twentieth century American society. Such various expressions as the report of the Harvard Committee on *General Education in a Free Society,* the programs of the progressive girls' colleges, the General College of Minnesota, and St. John's College in Maryland (whose curriculum represented a return to the *trivium* and *quadrivium* according to theories proposed by Robert Hutchins) have all been cited as examples of general education.

The argument that general education must be related to individual needs introduced the possibility that these experiences might contribute to vocational competency as well as to family life and citizenship. This, in turn, made it possible to argue that the qualities and abilities associated with general education could be developed equally well by vocational, preprofessional, physical

---

[14] Rudy, *op. cit.*

education, traditional liberal arts, or even shop courses. This enlarged conception of general education tended to equate it to contact with teachers having a general education—a self-defeating conception, for what faculty member would admit to not being generally educated?

Despite interest in general education, the major curricular trend in higher education up to World War II was toward the continuing expansion of offerings of frankly professional nature, even in the liberal arts colleges. Many new kinds of academic degrees were established, and the traditional baccalaureate came to acquire new forms. Richardson's study of private liberal arts colleges during the period 1890 to 1940 and Edwards' examination of the state universities within the area of the North Central Association both reported marked increase in the numbers of special baccalaureates.[15] Not only were the programs leading to these new degrees frankly professional, but the department literature also provided a long list of professions, occupational specialties, or graduate school possibilities that would be open to a student who majored in the field. The sciences have been prime offenders in this regard, but the humanities and the social sciences also follow the same practice in the hope of attracting a few more students.

In many cases, the solution to the problem of combining the liberal and the vocational has been resolved by extending the concept of major to include these fields. Thus, majors in business administration, secretarial studies, dramatic arts, music, and the like are now accepted as the equivalent of majors in more traditional departments for satisfying A.B. requirements. By this device, the liberal arts college achieved the pattern of undergraduate specialization characteristic of the university. The rapid development of these undergraduate professional specializations and the competition among institutions in establishing them led to the formation of organizations which attempted to set up accreditation requirements. Chemistry, medical technology, teaching, nursing, music, journalism are but a few of the fields for which such organizations have been formed. In this push to establish professional

---

[15] Orrin T. Richardson, "Requirements for Bachelor's Degrees, 1890–1940" (Doctor's thesis, University of Chicago, 1946), pp. 120-21, 147-59; and Harry F. Edwards, "Trends in the Development of the College Curriculum within the Area of the North Central Association, 1830–1930" (Doctor's thesis, University of Indiana, 1933), pp. 305–306.

quality, the tendency has been to expand the number of courses required and to outline in some detail the course content necessary for accreditation. This development further abetted specialization, enforced further expansion of courses in many institutions, and placed additional strictures on the faculty and students in curriculum planning.

The general education trend after World War I had frequently emphasized the development of broad interdisciplinary courses designed to give the students who took a limited amount of work in a particular area of knowledge an integrated overview of the essential ideas in that field. This pattern of interdisciplinary courses was resumed with renewed vigor after World War II. Such a course might be planned around the identification of major timeless problems, or the detailed study of a few major cultural epochs from which the current civilization has heavily drawn. Or it might be built around a few scientific theories carefully chosen to help the student achieve an insight into the nature of science without having to memorize the definitions, formulas, and all the tedious details of the typical introductory course. The extension of these broad interdisciplinary courses to the advanced level was promoted by the increasing awareness that the distinctions between the disciplines have tended to blur or to disappear on many of the research frontiers. There have appeared new departments, such as biochemistry, which involve some synthesis of hitherto separate courses.

The training of military personnel for warfare and for military government in various sections of the world during World War II, and our postwar international involvements, have accelerated the development of the area study concept in which the student specializes on an interdepartmental basis in the study of some major region of the world. Such college and university programs which feature a semester or a year of study in Europe, exchange students, exchange professors, and contracts for educational activity in far parts of the world, have given further impetus to area studies, concentrations, and course expansion. The college or university with an interest in a particular part of the globe soon finds itself offering courses in the history, geography, sociology, economics, religion, philosophy, and language of the area. The pressures toward this expansion are many. Many faculty members desire to travel, and how better to accomplish this than to make it apparent that one has a specialty that just must be used in a foreign area? When funds are being distributed for the development of such offerings and services, what department would be left out, thereby falling behind in growth or possibly being labeled as unprogressive? Finally, there is the possibility of attracting into a course the student who may not be interested in political science, history, philosophy, geography, psychology, as disciplines, but who may become interested in knowing more in detail about a particular area or country.

Because the student has no grasp of the basic disciplines involved, it is possible that such courses may degenerate into a guided tour of facts or that a program of concentration in an area study may become simply a compilation of introductory courses. Yet, in a manner reminiscent of the jubilant development of the elective system in the late nineteenth century, the expansion continues apace without much critical examination.

Shortly after 1950, it became apparent that higher education faces other problems which must be considered in curriculum development. There has been a marked expansion of the student population which will continue for some years. There is greater heterogeneity in the ability and in the interests of the students involved. Expansions in scientific research and technology are continually opening up specialties which seem to call for new patterns of preparation and often render archaic almost over night some of the existing curriculum patterns. International stresses and their impact on American democracy demand that education place far greater emphasis on non-Western cultures than ever before. There is increasing realization that humanities and social sciences must be reëmphasized and moral and spiritual values should be one of the fruits of higher education. The developing technology makes available to education new equipment, materials, and ideas which seemingly can improve the quality of education, at the same time making it feasible to serve the ever-increasing hordes of students. It is increasingly doubtful that the funds available to higher education, even with substantial federal subsidies in various forms, will keep pace either with the increase in the student body or with the increase in demands for services and new types of professional and vocational programs. There is some evidence that many professional and technical specialties are recognizing that the rapidity of change requires a return to emphasis on the fundamentals, or broad principles, and on the abilities to apply these in solving problems and reaching decisions. The detailed, how-to-do-it pattern, of course, can never quite keep up with the times. It becomes increasingly clear that course proliferation tends to result in small classes, heavy instructional loads, and high costs, as well as being a continuing source of disunity in the curriculum.

Summary

The institutions which make up American higher education are diverse in nature and take pride in this diversity. The diversity arises out of many factors. The American system of higher education drew principally on the English system in the development of the undergraduate college, and on the German system in the development of the graduate school. Scottish and French influences are also apparent. Colleges in various sections of the country inevitably took on the distinctive characteristics of their clientele and locale. Social pressures, technological needs for specialized personnel, and the expansion of knowledge have all contributed to the evolution of the essential character of higher education.

There have also been continuing quarrels as to whether higher education should be essentially a disciplinary experience or an opportunity for freedom of exploration by the individual; whether it should be designed for the intellectual élite or for a wide range of intellectual abilities and socio-economic backgrounds; and whether it should be oriented to the past, present, or future. It is difficult to trace definite trends, for colleges are at different stages of development with regard to any one issue and may even be moving in different directions. At a time when some colleges are still developing the elective idea and extending vocational offerings, St. John's College indicates a clearly retrogressive movement to the curriculum of the 1840–70 period. The following generalizations do clearly emerge:

1. In the short run, colleges may resist external demands for curricular change. But in the long run the program of the college and the university tends to be molded to a great extent by the demands of the supporting clientele.

2. Every occupational specialty and business or industry finds a degree of prestige associated with the existence in the college or university of a curriculum identified as preparatory to that field, and thus the pressures for expansion continue. Each such curricular expansion further underlines the trend toward a blending of vocational and liberal goals in education.

3. With colleges increasing in size and a resulting increase in the number of professors in any particular department, there is less and less tendency to define the merits of an educational program in terms of contact with particular individuals. Thus the course and credit pattern is further reinforced. Both professor and student increasingly tend to see the course as an end in itself rather than as one of the blocks out of which a total curricular experience is built.

4. The problem of physical plant space and pressures for fuller utilization of it are gradually forcing colleges to reëxamine the original concept of the residence college and consider whether or not the residence hall itself can be made more of an academic and learning center, with consequent improvement of relationships between faculty and students, enhancement of the academic atmosphere, and better all-around utilization of space. The same pressure for space forces institutions into thinking about year-around operations.

5. The use of tests has come to play an increasing role in higher education. Their use has made very clear that students at the beginning of their college education vary extremely in their background. The possibility of acceleration becomes, then, a means of recognizing student differences, and increasing the effective utilization of space by making it possible to care for more students. To the extent, then, that tests can be constructed which will determine whether or not an individual has had the equivalent of particular courses, there is increasingly widespread acceptance of the view that the student should receive credit and be permitted to move ahead at a rate determined by his own interests, ability, and application. This, in turn, tends to support the contentions of student personnel workers, evaluators, psychologists, and others who have argued that the significance of an educational program must be determined not simply by its structure or the processes it involves, but rather by its impact on individuals.

CHAPTER II

Basic Considerations
in Curriculum Planning[1]

Learning must be given direction, meaning, and organization by objectives which relate each unit and course to other courses and to the curriculum, or it degenerates to emphasis on isolated bits of information the importance and ultimate utility of which are not only unknown but must remain unquestioned. The extensive attention given to objectives in American higher education has had relatively minor impact on the planning of the educational experiences of students. The difficulty is not a lack of objectives but a failure to state and pursue meaningful ones. Objectives which are to give direction and coherence to the educational process must first be carefully selected and then defined as the bases for selection of materials and methods and ultimately as the bases for evaluation.

The Purposes and Functions of Higher Education

Certain terms recur in discussions of objectives. The purposes of colleges, as stated in college catalogs, charters, and presidential addresses, are reiterations of those broad educational ends to which colleges and universities are committed. Recurring and often trite words and phrases such as *character, well-rounded personality, philosophy of life* and *Christian ethic* sound highly desirable but provide no direct guidance in planning curriculum and instruction. Indeed, faculties and students are sometimes unaware of these statements which are aimed more at impressing the public than at guiding educational planning.

In a pluralistic society one can scarcely expect—indeed it is probably even undesirable—to find unanimity in educational phi-

---

[1] For an elaboration of the ideas presented in this chapter, see Dressel, *et al., Evaluation in Higher Education* (Boston: Houghton Mifflin Co., 1961), Chaps. 2 and 3.

losophy. Nevertheless, there must be some clearly defined purposes, objectives, or goals which give direction to the growth of the educational institution and which make it possible to develop a coherent and consistent program with a unity apparent to students, to faculty, and to the clientele generally. The preparation of a statement of purposes which outlines directions of development requires thoughtful consideration of the future as well as critical examination of the past.

Those purposes which are implicit in the present program may need to be made explicit and then accepted or rejected. Inconsistencies, confusion, or lack of coherence in courses, curriculum, student services, or budgetary emphases must be eliminated. Consideration of the evidence or lack of evidence as to the accomplishment of avowed purposes may indicate that the purposes are unclear or unachievable, or that unintended and even undesirable purposes are being attained. The clarification of purposes should be accompanied by specification of evidence accepted as relevant for determination of their attainment. When such specification is not possible, the purposes are not sufficiently clear to provide that direction and unity of effort which should be their major function. The program will then not be consistent with its purpose; day-to-day decisions will arise out of momentary expediency, and resources will not be wisely used. One source of difficulty lies in the failure to distinguish carefully among purposes, functions, and objectives. The distinctions which follow are undoubtedly somewhat arbitrary, but they are useful.

The *purposes* of higher education are generally recognized as at least threefold: to preserve the cultural heritage; to pass on the cultural heritage; and to augment, organize, and utilize that heritage. All institutions of higher education share these purposes, although research is especially a commitment of the university. More specific purposes only make explicit the particular aspects of that heritage for which an institution assumes responsibility.

The term *functions* includes those provisions, methods, or procedures whereby the purposes are to be achieved. Thus colleges provide instruction and courses in order to organize and pass on systematically the accumulating cultural heritage; they support libraries, museums, and scholars engaged in preserving and organizing this heritage; and they support research to discover new knowledge and to expand, add meaning to, and synthesize that heritage. Most colleges and universities—especially the land-grant institutions—accept responsibility for service functions and organize units and assign personnel to accomplish the purpose of putting knowledge to practical use. Clarification and evaluation of purposes and of functions are important and recurring tasks. One reason is that functions are sometimes added which are irrelevant to purposes. Thus it is difficult to relate emphasis on athletics to the purposes of higher education. Another reason is that institutions may change and, in so doing, may take on new purposes and functions. Thus colleges become universities and thereby accept responsibility for research. Still another reason is that the range of knowledge is so great that no institution can hope to achieve the several purposes in all areas.

The Objectives of Higher Education

Objectives, in contrast with purposes, are more explicit statements descriptive of the competencies and the traits which a program purports to develop in students. Objectives are especially related to the purpose of passing on the cultural heritage, but have relevance to other purposes as well, for individuals must be educated to continue pursuit of all the purposes in the future. The obligation to pass on the cultural heritage implies that students not only *know* the essentials of that heritage but that they also develop certain abilities and accept certain values which make that heritage useful to them and to their society. *Objectives* and *outcomes* are not synonymous. An *objective* states a desired outcome of education. Actual outcomes may or may not be identical with objectives, for educators seldom achieve all that they aim to achieve, and they may even achieve something quite different from what they are seeking. It can only be hoped that objectives will be reflected in outcomes. Outcomes may even come to influence objectives since there is no point in stating objectives which are unrealistic and impossible of achievement.

Objectives must provide direction, motivation, and organization or unity to the learning experiences planned for students. Therefore, the objectives must guide the instructor, both in deciding what and how to teach and in evaluating student accomplishments.

Objectives, to be effective, must define the student behavior which is desired and must define it in such a way that it can be identified as it develops. Highly complex, general, or ultimate goals descriptive of behavior in the years after college do not serve these purposes. Simple, immediate, and achievable objectives tend to be excessive in number and are equally ineffective. Objectives must be explicit but they must also be implicit in the activities demanded of students. To a degree, the expected behavior should be intrinsic in these activities, but objectives must also transcend daily activities in order to provide meaning and organization by relating these activities to the behaviors which the students are to develop. If objectives are clearly conceived, if they are understood and accepted by both faculty and students, and if they are reflected in the curriculum, then and only then will they fulfill their directive and unifying role.

Bases for the derivation and revision of objectives. Educational objectives, whatever their form, are derived from a limited number of sources. Education, as an instrument for the perpetuation and improvement of society, is necessarily responsive to the needs of the society in which it is imbedded. Conservative, classically oriented scholars may abhor this fact, but historical and current events demonstrate its accuracy. Whether educators consciously sense needs and respond to them or whether they wait until inexorable pressures force change, education does change. Narrow preoccupation with Western culture long characterized American thinking about liberal education, but educators have been shocked into the awareness that there are other cultures of equal significance. Education for contemplation has long since been overshadowed—even in the liberal arts colleges—by the necessity for earning a living. A flexibility permissive of continuing reasoned change is preferable to a rigidity spasmodically sent into convulsions by the necessity of changes which are then reluctantly assimilated into a new rigidity.

In a democracy, the needs of individuals must be considered as at least equal in weight to those of society. The extent to which education focuses on common needs of all students or on individual variants is a choice to be faced in each college. Institutions of higher education collectively disagree and individually vacillate as to the range of student needs for which they accept responsibility.

Shall the intellect be the sole concern or shall health and personality development be given equal emphasis?

A third source of objectives is found in the authoritative statements of individuals, conferences, professional organizations and their committees. Some professors and presidents apparently believe there has been no significant statement on education since Aristotle and Plato. Others are influenced by St. Thomas Aquinas, Milton, Newman, and even more recent writers. Reports of the various presidential commissions in higher education have left their mark.[2] The objectives and content of mathematics and physics courses are currently being rewritten by scholars in these disciplines.[3] For some teachers, unaware of all these influences, the textbook of the moment becomes, by default, the authority for both objectives and content.

From these three sources—needs of society, needs of the individual, and authority—a large and varied array of objectives will usually be derived. Some screening on the basis of psychological knowledge and philosophical points of view is necessary if the set of objectives finally chosen are to be (1) reasonable in number; (2) consistent with each other; (3) of approximately the same level of generality or specificity; (4) different or distinctive, but recognizing the complex nature of human behavior not usually completely independent; (5) descriptive of goals verifiably achievable by the means at hand.

Psychological research does not yet provide anything like full insight into human learning, but some principles are known and these offer some guidance in selection of objectives. Although Thorndike's position on the possibility of transfer was perhaps extreme, it is now accepted that objectives based on a generalized mental discipline and unlimited transfer are no longer sound. Psychological studies also suggest that objectives specifying inculcation of neatness or of desirable health habits are not adapted to

---

[2] *Higher Education for American Democracy,* Vol. I, "Establishing the Goals." A Report of the President's Commission on Higher Education (Washington, D.C.: U.S. Government Printing Office, 1947); see also, *Second Report to the President,* President's Committee on Education Beyond the High School (Washington, D.C.: U.S. Government Printing Office, 1957).

[3] *A Summary of the Report on Mathematics* (New York: College Entrance Examination Board, 1959); and *First Annual Report of the Physical Science Study Committee,* Vol. I, Preliminary Edition (Cambridge, Mass.: The Committee, 1958).

the level of maturity of college students. Such habits, however, may be indirectly required or reinforced by objectives more appropriate to the age level of college students.

Objectives might reasonably result from an accepted philosophy of education, but this is not common. Within any faculty, diverse and usually not explicit philosophies exist. At best, a compromise eclectic philosophy may emerge from agreement on objectives. As this philosophy is made explicit, objectives must be reëxamined for consistency with that philosophy which, because of its eclecticism, may itself lack consistency. Only in a relatively few colleges with religious affiliations are religious dogma and philosophical tenets sufficiently explicit to determine objectives, and even this determination is more evident in theoretical discussion than in actual practice. Departmentalization, course proliferation, and specialization in sub-disciplines have fragmentized knowledge. Long lists of specific objectives, if not completely ignored, may also be broken into bits because of the apparently greater relevance of these bits to the specialized interests of the faculty in each of the several disciplines. Clearly stated, pervasive and integrative objectives provide a major antidote to this fragmentation. Some objectives are more important than others; these few must be sought out and pursued intensively in full confidence that successful pursuit of them will be attended by satisfactory achievement of other less important objectives. Knowledge is fragmented but the behavior of people need not be. By making this evident, objectives justify the attention given to them.

Evaluation is essential in the selection of objectives. Studies of needs and decisions as to those which education should espouse involve both systematic research and value judgments. Some choice must be made among the many authorities seeking to dictate the course of education, preferably by evaluation of the rationale and logic underlying the conflicting views. Review of the results of psychological research and of its relevance to educational planning constitutes a form of evaluation. Philosophical considerations, by their essential nature, involve and require consideration of values. If any of these factors are ignored, efforts at achieving functional objectives may be negated.

Stages in Curriculum Planning

The identification of stages in the development of a course or curriculum promotes an erroneous conception of the discreteness of the stages and of the inviolability of a particular sequence. Nevertheless, the identification of several stages aids in demonstrating both the interrelationship of program development and evaluation and the recurrent repetition of the stages in that development. Figure 1 suggests several stages and the complex relationships existing among them.

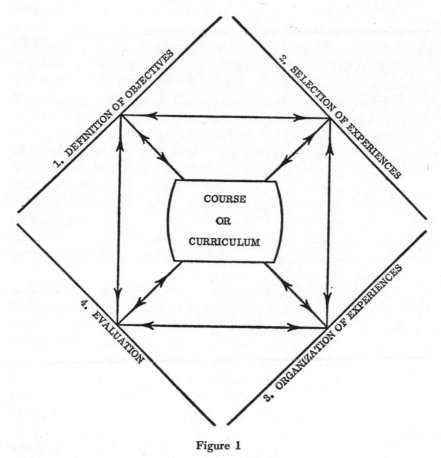

Figure 1

Once the decision to develop or to examine a course or curriculum is reached, the objectives should be formally stated. Educational experiences are selected as appropriate to the achievement of these objectives and the experiences are in turn organized in sequences to yield courses and curriculums. Appraisal of the effectiveness of the program in attaining its objectives may then produce evidence which results in revision of the program. This revision may involve alteration or replacement of any or all of the elements of the preceding stages: objectives, experiences, organization of the experiences, or even the evaluation procedures themselves. The presence of such continuing and thoughtful revision is essential if education is to remain a dynamic, stimulating enterprise.

Although Figure 1 is helpful in depicting the stages in development of an educational program, it has deficiencies. One of the more serious ones is the failure to exhibit the essential role that evaluation plays in the other three stages.

Another deficiency of Figure 1 is that it may be too readily interpreted as applicable only to the formal curriculum. Faculty and administrators must recognize that every practice and policy of a college affects the learning of students. Priorities in expenditures of funds reveal values of boards and administrators and thereby influence the values of students. Scholarship and loan policies, preferential treatment of athletes, social regulations, student government, and all other aspects of an institution constitute educational experiences. As such, they are subject to the analysis presented here, but the commitment of this monograph precludes more than passing attention to other than the formally organized curriculum.

Definition of objectives. It has already been stated that objectives may be derived from the needs of students, from the needs of society, and from authoritative statements of the purposes of education, with further examination and screening by reference to an educational philosophy and to known principles of learning.

A need, simply defined, is a discrepancy between the characteristics which students presently have and the characteristics which it is judged they ought to have. The determination of characteristics presently possessed by students is a research task and not a simple one. The characteristics which students ought to have is a matter of judgment and not one which the faculty or the individual instructor should lightly surrender to the student. Nevertheless, the latter must certainly be involved, for needs which are not originally discerned by the student must finally be understood and accepted by him, else he will be a reluctant accomplice in his own education.

The needs of students, thus viewed, are not antithetical to, or even separate from, the needs of society. A judgment about the characteristics which the individual ought to have must be made with reference to the society in which that individual is immersed. Whereas a static society reflects an all-pervasive demand to maintain the status quo, a dynamic society involves a continuing ferment and possibility of change the direction of which is never entirely predictable. Thus, some individual needs, which may appear at a given moment antithetical to the demands of a society, may be—in the long run—essential to the further evolution of that society. The society which does not permit individuals to examine critically its taboos and mores not only frustrates the individual who feels the need to do so, but also destroys its own capacity to adjust to changing circumstances. Social need rather than professional privilege is the justification for academic freedom.

It is an article of faith in a pluralistic, democratic society that the fullest development of the individual leads to the best and fullest development of the society. Nevertheless, the fullest development of the individual must always be viewed in relation to the society of which he is a part. The social misfit or reject seldom gains much satisfaction from life, and his immediate contribution to and influence upon society are reduced by his isolation. Clearly, it is necessary to consider needs both from the standpoint of the individual and from the standpoint of society; judgments about the one require consideration of the other. Balance is desirable, and it should be a balance resulting from awareness that objectives may determine whether education is to perpetuate the current society or produce individuals who are capable of developing a better one.

Any society includes many institutions, each of which meets certain social and personal needs. The generally accepted purposes and functions of higher education demonstrate that this social institution exists to meet some needs and not others. By attempting to do too much, higher education fragments its limited resources and does nothing very well.

In selecting objectives, some hierarchy of needs must be established. For present purposes, four stages in this hierarchy may be identified. The first level includes those needs which are explicit in the stated objectives of an institution. Knowledge, understanding, critical thinking, and communication of skills are not always recognized as needs by the individual, but they are needs which society has accepted and has charged to the university. In this first level, too, would be placed an awareness of values and the development in each student of some personal and ordered set of values. Instructional objectives, and objectives embodying the scholarly and research responsibilities of an institution also fall in this first category.

The second level of needs consists of those which might be called facilitating factors. For example, students need money to enter or remain in college; unless the student can find the money to remain in college, the college can have no effect on him. Hence, provision of scholarships, loans, and part-time work, and the academic and vocational counseling of students are evidently activities which meet some needs of students. Unless a student chooses his program wisely and sees some ultimate purpose in completing college, he is unlikely to remain. Commuting students, especially those in large urban universities, may make no demands which extend beyond these first two levels of need. They attend class, acquire credit, receive a degree, and are often self-sufficient otherwise—even to finding their own jobs after graduation.

The third level of student needs simply recognizes the inevitable concomitants of the continuing association of a sizable group of persons. The college or university in a small community must arrange for food and housing. Recreational facilities must usually be provided, either because the community does not provide such facilities in sufficient quantity or because the quality of those available is not consistent with the school's objectives. Thus most colleges arrange lectures, concerts, and other entertainment which provide students with recreational experiences not otherwise easily and cheaply available. Individual variation in interests (intellectual, aesthetic, or recreational) in any large group shortly gives rise to subgroups such as departmental clubs, social and religious groups, athletic teams, and journalistic enterprises. The activities which result from this third level of needs must be kept in proper perspective and so handled that student progress relative to objectives at the first level of need is reinforced rather than negated by these experiences.

The fourth level of needs is that for which a college must reject obligation. The college may refuse admission to individuals who require high-school-level remedial work or who possess undesirable personality characteristics. In rejecting a need, a college may assign the responsibility for meeting that need to the individual himself or to other agencies. The college does not knowingly admit criminals or psychotics because other social agencies are better equipped to educate such individuals. A college may also reject responsibility for a particular need by denying its significance. On many campuses, for example, students are denied the privilege of having a car, although, from the student's point of view, the need for transportation is an important one. Some colleges apparently regard discriminatory social groups (fraternities and sororities) as falling in this fourth level and accordingly ban them. A few colleges view intercollegiate athletics in the same light, although the intramural program is usually, and appropriately, regarded as falling in the third level.

Every college should examine the various needs of students and reach some accord on a hierarchical order. Unless this is done, the identification of a need dictates an objective and the introduction of a program to meet it. The new program competes with other functions for support and generates status needs in those assigned responsibility for it. These new functionaries soon begin to see their activity as an end in itself and may attempt to enlarge its scope and push it ever higher in the hierarchy. At times, the search for athletes has become so important as to make mockery of admissions and scholarship standards. The resulting lack of consistency between purposes and programs confuses students and generates more difficulties and needs. Student needs must be examined but the introduction of functions to meet every identified student need is quite unjustified.

Selection and planning of educational experiences. The triteness and seemingly obvious truth of the observation that people do not always learn by experience may blind one to the fact that this is the only way in which individuals do learn. Basically, the observation is false; the difficulty is that individuals do not always learn because the experiences were not carefully selected and planned with specific objectives in mind. The possible range of learning experiences is much greater than that actually used, as the following list indicates:

1. Materials (textbooks, supplemental required or optional readings, teaching machines, current periodicals, syllabi, slides, films, tapes, recordings, television).
2. Instructional methods (lectures, discussions, demonstrations, role playing, cases, problems, individual conferences, seminars, guest speakers, telephone interviews).
3. Assignments (readings, problems, papers, oral reports).
4. Activities (laboratory, field trips, observation, internships, work experience, travel, public lectures, concerts, plays).
5. Evaluation methods (objective tests, essays, papers, reports, participation, peer judgment, self-evaluation).

No one course of the common three- to five-credit variety extending over one quarter or one semester can effectively employ all the preceding experiences but, by noting them, the narrow conception of experiences upon which many courses are planned becomes apparent. Furthermore, the choice of experiences made by the instructor is often predicated upon his own activity rather than upon the objectives. Thus the instructor implies that what *he* does or says or what the textbook or other authority says is more important than what the *student* understands and concludes. The student then infers that his reactions and ideas are to be subjugated to the search for what the instructor wants. And thus the student may totally fail or only superficially succeed relative to desired objectives because he had no personal experience involving the objectives, but only an enforced sharing of experience with the instructor.

An accepted objective of instruction is the development of increased ability to relate ideas in solving a problem. It is desirable that the instructor present a model of this desired behavior, but continuing instructor presentation may only result in the student learning the instructor's organization and solution without himself developing much insight or any ability.

A limited conception of evaluation is that it "draws out" and makes evident the value in an educational experience. Unless evaluation has first been invoked to assure that the desired behaviors are implicit in the educational experience, evaluation of the outcomes of the educational experience is unlikely to be profitable. In selecting and planning experiences, questions will be raised and alternatives will be presented. Evaluation can and should play a major role in reaching decisions on these questions and alternatives.

The usual approach to evaluation of the worth of experiences is based upon consideration of the changes in students, but Wynne has argued that the objectives of general education are such that evaluation by study of student change is difficult or even impossible in any reasonable span of time.[4] From careful analysis of the objectives, he derives such characteristics as contingency, sociality, interest, originality, intelligence, and purpose. He then argues that if these characteristics are not present, the experiences are inadequate to the purposes. Although this type of evaluation savors somewhat of armchair rationalizing, it does provide some assurance that the experiences provided have some relevance to the objectives agreed upon. If evaluation is involved in planning the *process* of education, the evaluation of the *results* is much more likely to be positive.

Organization of experiences. There are many bases for organizing courses and curriculums. Some disciplines possess what appears to be an inherent logical order, although this may be historical accident rather than necessity. Other disciplines are exemplified by movement from the simple to the complex, from the specific to the general, or from the immediate to the more remote (in interest, in time, or in space). Some may be characterized by a reverse movement, as from the general to the specific. In history, for example, the more remote may precede the immediate.

In applying these or other principles of organization, essentially three criteria may be identified. There must be continuity: learnings provided by earlier experiences must be used in later ones. The full meaning and utility of any significant concept, value, or skill is not grasped upon first contact. Repetition is necessary for reinforcement. Sheer repetition, by its very monotony, may impede mastery, but repetition with deeper insight and an expanding range of association promotes learning. Continuity in learning must be abetted by sequence: the continuing use of an idea must proceed to even greater depth and complexity. This means that learning experiences should be so planned as to be cumulative rather than discrete.

---

[4] John P. Wynne, *General Education in Theory and Practice* (New York: Bookman Associates, 1952).

Finally, if the learning in a particular course or discipline is to take on its fullest meaning, it must be related to learning in other courses, other disciplines, and to experiences external to the classroom. Some writers on curriculum theory have labeled this last quality integration.[5]

These three criteria, *continuity, sequence,* and *integration,* should be utilized both in planning courses and in planning the total curriculum.

Evaluation. The preceeding paragraphs have argued that evaluation—the weighing and choosing of alternative objectives, experiences, and patterns of organization—is an essential part of each of these phases of curriculum development. Evaluation of the composite program by careful study of its impact on the students is necessary also. This impact can be measured only by comparing the students' status just before beginning the course or curriculum with their status at its conclusion. The changes noted may be taken as indicative of the effectiveness of the experiences. If alternative patterns of experience exist, crude comparisons of their relative effectiveness may be made by contrasting the changes noted under each pattern.

If little or no change is found to ensue, several possibilities must be considered: (1) the objectives may be inappropriate, unclear or unachievable; (2) the experiences may not be relevant to the objectives; (3) the organization of experiences may be inadequate; (4) the evaluation instruments may be invalid. After modifying one or more of these, the stage is set for repetition of the process.

Concepts Useful in Curriculum Planning

There are a number of concepts which are commonly used in discussing the problems of curriculum balance. These include *breadth, depth, prerequisites, sequences,* and *integration.* Although most of these terms have already been used, some additional discussion of them and of their interrelationships will be useful as a background for consideration of educational patterns and principles.

Depth. The depth component of education is usually achieved

---

[5] For an extended discussion of this concept and a comprehensive bibliography see *The Integration of Educational Experiences,* Fifty-seventh Yearbook of the National Society for the Study of Education, Part III, Nelson B. Henry, ed. (Chicago: University of Chicago Press, 1958).

through a departmental major or through a concentration built around some problem, geographical area, cultural group, or broad divisional grouping of disciplines. The conception of a double major, once popular in some colleges, has generally disappeared along with increases in major requirements. The minor too appears to be less used than formerly. Originally viewed as a supporting element in acquiring depth, the minor may now refer to a selection of courses less intensive than a major and completely unrelated to it. Specialization in an undergraduate vocational curriculum may be regarded as a major. Honors programs and independent study usually become means to even greater specialization, both in time spent and in narrowness of the problem studied, than the ordinary major.

Breadth. There are several distinctive concepts of breadth. One is that breadth is insured by requirements which bring the student into contact with the major divisions of knowledge. The obvious difficulty with this concept is that the possible divisions of knowledge are so many and the possible courses in each so diverse that either distribution requirements or a few required courses may degenerate into superficiality by attempting too much or covering too little.

A second conception of breadth is that the student should be brought into contact with the major problems that have concerned man throughout recorded history and with some of the solutions proposed or views held in regard to them. A specialized faculty member finds it difficult to deal with such problems, except as each is approached from his own specialized view; he is also distrustful of any attempt to provide this broad treatment.

A third conception of breadth, closely related to the second, is that a student should be brought into contact with systems of value and with cultures very different from his own in order that he may come to reflect upon and critically examine his own values and those of his culture. This conception has become more common in recent years because of the role of the United States in the international scene.

A fourth conception of breadth is that the student should come into contact with the distinctive methodology of the various disciplines. According to this view, it is more important that the nonscientist, for example, understand something of the nature of the scientific method than that he know any minimum amount of science. These last three conceptions of breadth appear superior to the first, which all too commonly results in a quick tour in which the existence of knowledge is realized but its essence is missed.

Prerequisites and sequences. Meaningful sequences can be developed only as subsequent courses are based upon preceding ones. The elective principle placed a premium on the student's freedom to take almost any course in which he might be interested. All prerequisites came under critical examination. In many cases, prerequisites had been unrealistic because they were defined entirely by references to specific courses rather than in terms of necessary competencies which a student might conceivably have developed from other courses or experiences. Thus the critical examination of prerequisites was a healthy move but too often resulted in departmental offerings having no sequential relationship to each other. Except in a few course areas—such as foreign languages, science, and mathematics, it became popular to offer courses at every level without specific prerequisites. With the discard of prerequisites and hence of the concept of sequence, the concept of depth, too, has been degraded to a matter of courses and hours or to some crude estimate of maturity as determined by the class level of the student. Senior courses, in too many cases, assume no more background than freshman courses do, and they may be intrinsically no more difficult, although the treatment in great detail of a narrow range of topics may give an illusion of greater depth.

The concept of sequence has relevance in regard to breadth as well as to depth. Indeed, the relationship of breadth to depth involves the idea of sequence. It is sometimes argued that breadth should precede depth—that is, that the first two years of college should aim at breadth, the last two at depth. It can also be argued that breadth and depth experiences should parallel and complement each other throughout the four years. Finally, it may be argued that the most meaningful breadth emerges out of a specialization which forces a realization that the study in depth of any discipline ultimately impinges upon all other areas of knowledge.

Integration. The discussion of sequential organization leads into the concept of integration. *Sequence* implies the building of one course on another in such a way that the first is preparatory to the second and the second builds upon and expands the ideas, concepts, and principles developed in the first. *Integration* implies both the interrelationship of disciplines and the application of the knowledge and principles of the several disciplines to problems and issues of society. Integration in the first sense was evident in the classical curriculum because students and professors shared a common educational experience, because each instructor taught all phases and levels of the curriculum, because religion played a major role in the curriculum, and because the prevalent view was that education consisted in mastering an already existent and fully integrated body of truth. Integration, in the sense of application to the problems of society, was hardly a concern, since the mental discipline concept of psychology assumed that a trained mind could cope with anything. Moreover, the problems of this world were considered to be, in a sense, of less concern than those of the next.

Integration can no longer be regarded as mastery of a fully organized and interrelated body of knowledge. The goal rather is the integrative mind which continually seeks knowledge and continually gains new insights into previous knowledge and into problems and experiences arising in all phases of his existence. Each individual must seek his own integration but education must help him in this task by discussion of the efforts of others, by instruction which models the integrative mind in action, and by tasks which permit and encourage the student to discover new relationships.

CHAPTER III

Some Curriculum Models, Underlying Philosophies, and Problems

Nonpreparatory liberal education. There are four somewhat distinctive types of undergraduate programs. The first is liberal education of nonpreparatory nature. Actually, an education which is not in some way preparatory for something is difficult to imagine. The most ardent believer in "pure" liberal arts would agree that education should aid the individual to lead the good life and to become a better citizen. He might also agree that the liberal arts should contribute something to success in a vocation, even though this would be incidental and indirect. Good examples of nonpreparatory programs are not easy to find, for modern culture is not hospitable to them, but some characteristics associated with nonpreparatory liberal education can be identified.

Nonpreparatory liberal education requires the students and teachers to grapple with ideas of timeless import. It assumes that the understanding of these ideas and the concepts and principles involved in them will be relevant in the solution of many problems. There remains in this program a vestige of the mental discipline conviction that wrestling with these ideas will develop abilities applicable to the solution of any problem. Thus this concept of liberal education for its own sake without regard to utility is, in a sense, a concept of an education of maximal utility.

Preparation for graduate study. Closely related to the nonpreparatory concept of education, yet further demonstrating the lack of clarity in that concept, is undergraduate education pursued as preparation for graduate study. Undergraduates with a deep interest in knowledge for its own sake may nevertheless consider their undergraduate study to be preparatory. With the assistance of their advisers, they select courses which maximize opportunity for success in graduate school. Education pursued with this objective cannot reasonably be called nonpreparatory. The extent to which liberal arts college faculties take pride in the percentage of their protegés that go on to graduate school demonstrates their concern for preparatory rather than nonpreparatory education. Such devotion to graduate study can easily destroy the possibility of providing a broad, nonpreparatory liberal education.

Preprofessional undergraduate programs. A third type of undergraduate program, regarded as quasi-liberal in nature by its almost universal presence in the liberal arts college, is preprofessional education. Professional schools in law, medicine, and dentistry arose initially outside of the colleges and universities (see Chapter I) but now are most commonly associated with them. These professional schools have gradually come to require that applicants have an extensive undergraduate education. This requirement arises out of two mutually supporting and yet partially contradictory considerations.

A liberal education requirement acts as a selective factor, adding prestige to the profession, and enabling the professional man to fulfill more ably influential community roles unrelated to his specialized education. Some areas of professional concern—for example, the physician's concern with socialized medicine—may also extend into areas for which the purely technical education does not provide adequate insight. Thus, the professional man needs frequently to be a liberally educated person in the fullest meaning of that phrase.

On the other hand, the amount of science which a physician must know has increased far beyond what a strictly professional training can encompass and still do justice to the necessary professional competencies. Accordingly, professional education has demanded more preparation in those arts or science fields immediately relevant to the professional studies. Liberal requirements may thereby become preprofessional and preparatory.

Occupational curriculums. Another type of undergraduate program is found in the avowedly occupational training curriculum. This type may be broken down into subtypes according to the number of years required and the relative emphases on liberal and occupational work. Curriculums in engineering, agriculture, home economics, and business have typically become four-year degree programs although the requirements—especially in engineering—

may greatly exceed those of the usual four-year program. The proportions of these curriculums which can be regarded as non-occupational or liberal vary from institution to institution.

The definition of "liberal" is also important in determining the proportion. Thus, the typical engineering school of the four-year pattern requires a year of freshman English. If this is the same course as is required of all other students, it may readily be accepted as a liberal arts element in the experience of the engineer. When offered by a special staff of teachers associated with the college of engineering, its liberal education quality may come into question, for competency in the writing of technical reports can too easily become the most obvious objective.

Mathematics and the sciences pose a somewhat different problem. Mathematics, for example, is so basic to the field of engineering that, even when the engineering student takes his mathematics with other students, there is a possibility that his personal motivation will overshadow the possible liberal overtones of the course experience. If special mathematics or science sections are offered for the engineering student, and especially if these are taught by persons on the engineering faculty, the possibility is even greater that these courses will acquire a more technical nature. A social science or humanities sequence has less direct relevance to engineering, and the choice of topics for treatment cannot so easily be subverted to the needs of the engineering profession. Thus, in the four-year occupational programs, there is a continuum of possible course experiences ranging from courses planned and offered in a truly liberal vein, through semiprofessional or preprofessional courses with specific relevance to the field, to courses designed specifically to promote proficiency in the occupation.

The academic respectability of some of the technical courses required is dubious. For example, four-year secretarial training programs usually include credit courses in typing, shorthand, filing, and the like. These courses differ in no significant respect from those offered in secondary schools or in business colleges, and there is no significant body of knowledge for the student to master. In home economics, great emphasis has been placed on sewing and cooking. Engineering curriculums have included mechanical drawing and shop work. The current trend is toward the elimination of such skills courses from college degree programs. In part, this trend results from doubt as to the appropriateness of these courses in college, and is in part redefinition of the technical field at a higher level.

General comments on vocational curriculums. The issue has been and will be long debated as to what occupational knowledge and competencies are appropriate for a four-year degree diploma. The view that all professional training should be postponed to the post-baccalaureate period is not likely to meet with widespread acceptance. Community colleges and technical institutions may take over responsibility for post-high school occupational training which does not require sustained contact with one or more of the disciplines offered in four-year colleges. But as these terminal program occupations attain a measure of acceptance and prestige by requiring post-high school education, there will be a tendency for the occupations involved to insist on a college degree program. Colleges and universities will need to screen such demands and yet avoid an arbitrary negative position which would interfere with the natural growth of new and needed specialties. The history of such fields as teacher education, medical technology, nursing, and journalism (to take but a few examples) is instructive in this regard.

One of the difficulties in planning occupational programs is found in the lack of clarity in the titles. "Home economics," "engineering," and other occupational terms have very different levels of meaning. These levels of meaning have developed gradually, so that the layman—and even some of the professionals trained in an earlier period—are not sensitive to the change or to the need for carefully differentiating occupational roles and related educational programs. The various tasks and levels of proficiency in some of these fields need to be studied and some principles derived whereby college degree programs for occupational fields are truly distinctive in the experiences required and the kind of behavior anticipated. In engineering, for example, it is evident that modern technology demands college-trained engineers who are qualified to move into supervisory and planning positions. There will frequently be little concern as to whether the graduate is a civil, mechanical, electrical, or chemical engineer. This would seem to justify emphasis on the essential principles of mathematics and sciences and on ideas common to all engineering fields, with more specialized work relegated to graduate study or practical experience.

It has already been noted that the several occupational curriculums in four-year colleges vary markedly in the weighting of liberal and purely vocational education requirements. They vary also in the assignment of courses to these two phases of education. Journalism is perhaps at one extreme; for, if the recommendations of the journalism accrediting associations were followed, journalism courses would constitute no more than 25 per cent of the student's undergraduate program. The other 75 per cent of his work would be in a broad, liberal education emphasizing the social sciences. Any attempt to offer special English or social science for journalists would fail of producing what is really demanded—a liberally-educated person who is especially interested in helping others to become informed about and understand what is happening in the world. There are, however, skills and facts about the operation of communication media which are highly desirable for the novice in the journalism field. There are also ethical and legal considerations of which he should be aware. These topics provide the basis for a small and academically respectable set of requirements which may, if they are offered by liberally-educated journalism professors, reinforce the liberal education experience provided in the nonvocational part of the student's program.

Engineering perhaps exemplifies the other extreme. In the four-year curriculum, not more than 25 per cent of the undergraduate program can be regarded as liberal in nature, and relatively few four-year programs contain that much. Between these two extremes is to be found a wide range of four-year programs which purport to turn out a liberally-educated individual qualified to take a position in a particular occupational field.

The rationale for the specific requirements in vocational curriculums often does not stand up well under critical examination. In analyzing some occupational field, the advice of persons in the field plus the composite judgment of the teaching staff may result in consensus that "dealing with people" is an important component. This is too readily equated to the requirement of a course in personnel psychology developed about a special selection of problems and a prescribed pattern of procedures for dealing effectively with them. The result is that the student is deprived of the opportunity to master basic concepts and principles and fails to develop any ability to apply these in new and unforeseen circumstances.

The emphasis on preprofessional and occupational programs in college catalogs causes students to consider them as the preferred pattern. Statements regarding liberal education are obscured by this emphasis. The specific rules about liberal education which do appear, by focusing on courses and credit requirements, may fail to communicate its nature or worth. Departmental statements and advisory practices do little to counteract this general impression. Thus the student who does not have a definite vocational goal around which to plan his curriculum is viewed—and may view himself—as unusual, odd, or abnormal.

Patterns Observable
in the Liberal Arts Colleges

Current developments point up the decline of pure liberal education. The well-documented trend in the liberal arts college has been in the direction of an increase in departments and courses. The specialized education of the graduate school has contributed heavily to this.

The combination of a large number of liberal arts departments and of a number of preprofessional and occupational curriculums makes it very difficult to achieve any unity or even significant sharing of educational experiences in the undergraduate curriculum. If general requirements applicable to all degrees become extensive, requests are soon made for a waiver of some of these for special programs. The department of music, which takes its greatest pride in its highly specialized majors in applied music, is one of the first to seek relief. Once exceptions are made, it is difficult to hold the line with other groups who also see perfectly good reasons why certain requirements should be eliminated. The tendency may then be to set up a common but very limited general set of requirements for all curriculums.

Countermeasures. There have been countermeasures in the liberal arts colleges. Broad, introductory general education courses and more advanced interdisciplinary offerings have been introduced. Because these courses draw upon such a wide range of material, it is difficult to obtain agreement on their content and to find instructors who feel competent to teach them. Even in the small liberal arts college, the individual who engages in this activity may feel or be made to feel by his colleagues that this assignment is less desirable than teaching courses of the more traditional pattern. Such broad courses do not fit into the departmental structure, and this may place instructors involved in them in a much less secure position than their departmental colleagues. Subjected to the doubts and criticisms of the departmentalized component of the staff, these individuals are more dependent on the whims of administration for promotion and recognition. Moreover, they reasonably fear that they may jeopardize their possibility of moving to other institutions because their affiliation with a particular discipline has been clouded by their interdisciplinary efforts. There is also difficulty in relating these courses to departmental offerings. Duplication between the broad general courses and the introductory departmental courses encourages continuous debate as to whether the student planning to major in the field should or should not take the broad general education course inclusive of the area of his special interest.

A few institutions offer a series of courses developed around broad problems or issues. In such courses, content is introduced as it has relevance to the problem at hand. The education of college teachers does not prepare them for this interdisciplinary, problem-oriented teaching and the usual instructional load provides neither the time nor the encouragement to develop such courses. The use of an interdisciplinary team of teachers can be successful but may only fragment the course as each overemphasizes his own special interests and, at the same time, greatly increase the total teaching load. One of the prime examples of this type of course—the integrative senior seminar—has met with mixed responses from faculties and has had spotty success.[1]

The concentration area has also seen some experimentation in recent years. Interdisciplinary research emphasizes the necessity for seeking new interrelationships in the various disciplines. This, in turn, has made it acceptable to consider depth experiences not necessarily confinable to a single department. The difficulty in planning such a concentration by use of existing courses, however, must not be minimized. There is too frequently a lack of sequence within departments, and therefore lack of cumulative and significant

---

[1] W. Hugh Stickler, "Senior Courses in General Education," *Journal of Higher Education*, XXV, No. 3 (March 1954).

depth experience even for a major. When an array of courses is selected from a number of different departments, the problem is greatly increased. In some institutions, such broad concentrations are accompanied by an insistence on some amount of independent study by the student. This provision seems wise, especially if it encourages efforts to integrate the formal course experiences.

In some liberal arts colleges, the divisional organization has been introduced as one way to break down departmentalization and provide a home for the somewhat broader general education or interdisciplinary course. Another and even more popular counter-measure to excessive departmentalization is the comprehensive examination. These are offered at various levels and are of many different types. The two most frequently found are at the end of the sophomore and the senior years. The first generally serves the purpose of checking on the breadth component of liberal education by requiring that the student demonstrate not only that he has an adequate knowledge of the several fields, but that he has some perception of relationships among them, and perhaps even some ability to apply principles or ideas from these fields to new problems or situations. At the senior level, the comprehensive examination may be departmental, or it may be extended to include divisional and even broader general or liberal education components. The anticipated role of the comprehensive examination is that of keeping before both students and faculty the importance of certain broad educational purposes or goals which transcend specific courses or individual departments. Comprehensive examinations have been highly successful in some institutions and, as a result, have been adopted elsewhere. But without careful analysis of its relationship to the total four-year experience, the comprehensive examination becomes a meaningless and irritating additional hurdle. An examination at the senior level cannot ask the student to do truly comprehensive tasks unless his prior educational experience has been so planned as to require them of him.

Many colleges with programs having unique and highly interesting elements could be cited but, waiving minor variations (dear as they may be to the individual colleges), the most common pattern is a three-fold requirement. The student is required to have contact with a number of different fields through a distribution requirement. He is required to take certain specific courses such as English composition and foreign languages. Finally he is required to complete a major. The most common alternative to the distribution requirement is a number of broad interdisciplinary courses which are offered either as options or as general requirements.

The requirement in freshman composition has been described at times as the only common requirement in colleges and universities, although the fact is that there are a few exceptions. Despite the widespread continuance of the requirement, there is no great satisfaction with it. Communication skills are broad objectives which should be of concern in all college courses. So long as the responsibility for writing or other communication skills is assigned to a single course at the freshman year, it may be expected that the dissatisfaction will continue. Typically, English departments have the responsibility for this course, but they are not always well prepared to fulfill it. The staff is generally trained in highly specialized aspects of literature; some of the teachers are relatively uninterested in the expository writing with which the majority of the other departments are concerned. Perhaps one of the best solutions is to base the course on some substantive body of knowledge or on ideas not adequately covered elsewhere and yet of general interest to students. This provides a significant set of ideas upon which the student can write and crystallize some of his own thoughts. Moreover, as at the College of Wooster where this first course deals with the nature of a liberal education, teachers from departments other than English may be recruited. When such a content base is introduced, however, there is a risk that some instructors will become more interested in content coverage than in the teaching of writing.

Foreign languages are an anachronism today. Originally, the classics were the core of the liberal arts program. Competency in Greek and Latin was assumed, and the classics were read for the ideas therein, rather than to increase competency in the language. As the student population increased, and more and more students came with inadequate preparation, emphasis tended to be placed on mastery of grammar and on translation. The introduction of modern languages found justification in the need for understanding the culture of other nations, but the lack of prior contact with the language usually required attention to grammar and the development of some competency in reading. During and after World War

II, attention came to be focused on oral facility. Many institutions have moved from a requirement specified in terms of courses and credits to a requirement defined by proficiency as measured by an examination.

Philosophy and religion have an important role in the curricular requirements of many religiously affiliated liberal arts colleges. Not infrequently, both the extent of these requirements and the dogmatic approach to them destroy the possibility of adequate breadth and the essential spirit of a liberal education. This area, however, is a sensitive one, and such requirements are neither readily modified nor even critically examined.

Most of the problems which have been presented here in connection with a liberal arts college also have relevance for that unit of the university which still purports to offer the opportunity for liberal education. One might be tempted to assume that the solutions would be more easily found in the relatively uncomplicated liberal arts college. Yet liberal arts colleges too have their pressures and their conflicts.

Patterns Observable in the University

The autonomy accorded institutions of higher learning in America extends, at least for private institutions, to choice (by the governing board) of designation as college or university. The rapidity with which land-grant colleges and teachers' colleges have, in recent years, become state universities suggests that legislatures, too, are far more generous with the title "university" than with the appropriations needed to make the title meaningful. As an institution of "complex structure," the university usually has a greater number of departments than a liberal arts college has and introduces, in addition, divisions, schools, colleges, institutes, and centers offering a wide range of courses and of professional and technical curriculums. Some of the latter, such as the packaging curriculum offered in one institution, can only cause astonishment and chagrin to those for whom the term "higher education" has intellectual implications.

While permitting some choice in courses, the range of offerings in the typical liberal arts college department usually is restrained to what might be described as a single major. In the university, a single department may offer a range of courses wide enough to support five or six completely distinctive majors. Curriculums involving course offerings from several colleges or departments further increase the number of alternatives available.

But the organization of the university also adds complications. Whereas the liberal arts college, in theory at least, is unitary in nature and specifies several degree requirements applying to all candidates, the undergraduate schools and colleges found in universities may have considerable autonomy in specifying requirements. The type of university which is made up of a number of graduate professional schools surrounding one undergraduate college may enforce fairly universal requirements, but the typical state university with numerous co-equal colleges finds the establishment of general undergraduate requirements well-nigh impossible. Freshman composition and physical education (with or without credit) and a minimum credit requirement for a degree may be the only specifications. Thus the actions at the University of Florida and at Michigan State University in establishing a University College and a set of general education courses required of all students must be considered a tribute to effective administrative leadership.

The presence of a graduate school also influences the undergraduate program of the university. In a growing university, no department in the arts, letters, social science, or science fields will long be content to offer only undergraduate work, for the failure to offer the master's degree and the doctorate makes it difficult to hire a strong faculty, and renders the staff relatively powerless—both in the university and in the various professional organizations.

This preoccupation with expansion into graduate work pushes undergraduate teaching into a secondary role. If it were not that undergraduate instruction provides leverage for increasing the number of positions in a department, it would receive even less attention. Undergraduate instruction at the lower divisional level often provides financial support for graduate students. Furthermore, a large undergraduate enrollment justifies increasing the full-time faculty, which, in turn, makes it possible to cover more effectively the various subspecialties of the discipline.

In a university department which is just developing its program of graduate study, the junior- and senior-level offerings often reflect an unreasonably high degree of specialization because these courses can be used to attract graduate students, while a respectable enrollment can be maintained by encouraging, if not demanding, enrollment by undergraduate students. As a result of the abuse of this pattern in many universities, the college of literature, science, and arts is actually the most professionalized unit in the university.[2]

Whereas the departments in the various professional colleges are at least held together by the common concern about the broad professional field for which they are responsible, the several departments of the college of science and arts each exult in their independence and gauge their success by the number of students they are able to enroll in the graduate program. Introductory courses in these departments are not infrequently taught by the less qualified members of the staff, and the courses may be oriented to the needs of the student who concentrates in the area. Complaints (not always justified) from other departments and colleges regarding inadequacy of these course offerings are often ignored, with the result that the complaining department presents a competing course in disguised form. Such duplication in course offerings is rampant in many universities. Courses in statistics, genetics, and marriage may be offered in as many as half a dozen departments. The threat of duplication, however, may cause a department to offer course variants especially tailored to the needs of several different curricular groups. Thus, slight variations in content, in credit hours, or in prerequisites may be the only distinctions between three, four, or more overlapping introductory courses. Such special courses, by selection of material and by segregation of students according to vocational interest, tend to replace liberal goals with vocational ones by placing emphasis on specific topics and skills rather than on basic concepts and principles. Unfortunately, another threat to the liberal education character of the introductory courses is their development as the initial step in departmental specialization, which, in turn, is viewed as a step toward graduate study.

Analyses of professional and technical curriculums generally conclude that a reorganization basing these curriculums more

---

[2] In one university excessive use of junior (300–399) and senior (400–499) courses for graduate credit led to faculty action debarring acceptance of 300 level courses for graduate credit. Within a year, many departments successfully renumbered almost all 300 courses at the 400 level so that they might still be used for graduate credit.

firmly on broad understandings and principles of the related liberal arts and sciences is desirable. Faculties of the professional and technical schools, however, commonly lack this type of education themselves. They need cooperation from their associates in the arts and sciences in planning courses which have meaning and relevancy for both majors and non-majors. Professional and technical faculties seem generally to be more interested and willing to work upon this problem than their colleagues in science and arts, all too many of whom take the view that criticism from students or faculty in vocational areas is only a reflection of the incompetency or practical orientation of the critics.[3]

Countermeasures. In addition to the countermeasures adopted by liberal arts colleges, universities have inaugurated others adapted to their size and complexity. One such measure has been the introduction of a lower division of either one or two years. Theoretically, this makes it possible to give more direct attention to the quality of freshman and sophomore work, and to provide competent counseling and faculty advising in what is, for many students, a period of vocational exploration. Unless the lower division has some direct control over instruction, either through responsibility for the planning and offering of a number of general education courses or through participation in the selection and reward of faculty teaching introductory courses, the director or dean of the lower division will find himself playing the role of a glorified clerk. Additional justification for the lower division or university college concept may be found in the next few years as more and more students transfer from the community-junior colleges. A transition from one unit to another within the university at the same level as the transfer from the community college could ease the establishment of admission policies and practices for admission to the junior year.

The University of South Florida has a College of Basic Studies which offers seven basic studies, six of which all students must complete. In addition, this college offers a senior "capstone" course and an upper division program of integrated studies leading to a

---

[3] Paul L. Dressel, Lewis B. Mayhew, and Earl J. McGrath, *The Liberal Arts as Viewed by Faculty Members in Professional Schools* (New York: Teachers College, Columbia University, 1959); and Paul L. Dressel and Margaret F. Lorimer, *The Attitudes of Liberal Arts Faculties Toward Liberal and Professional Education* (New York: Teachers College, Columbia University, 1960).

major in basic studies. Other universities have provided for alternatives to the departmental major by means of divisional majors or a special department of liberal studies (University of Washington).

Wesleyan University in Connecticut has introduced a number of independent college units in the several divisional areas of knowledge. This move illustrates one means whereby the large American university might subdivide into a number of college units, thus providing all the advantages of the small liberal arts colleges and all of the advantages—in terms of resources—of a university. This pattern, similar to that of the English university, deserves more exploration and attention than it has thus far received. Still another pattern is suggested by the division of the College of Science and Arts at Michigan State University into three colleges: Social Sciences, Sciences, and Arts and Letters. The expectation is that each of these new units will develop a broad liberal education degree as well as the more specialized departmental majors and that each unit will also be able to relate itself more effectively to the several vocational colleges or schools which depend heavily upon it for the basic training of their students.

Unity in the Undergraduate Program

At no point is greater difference found in educational philosophies than in the views as to how unity is to be achieved in the undergraduate program. Hong and his associates at St. Olaf's College have provided a helpful analysis of four major concepts of integration or unity in higher education.[4] They note that one widely prevalent view, additive in nature, really begs the question of unity by assuming that no unity exists in qualitatively describable terms. Each course is interchangeable with any other course, providing only that the course units or credits are the same. With only a few restrictions on selection of courses, grade average, and upper division credits, the degree is awarded a student when the number of courses or course units reaches some specified total. This conception lends itself nicely to multiplication of departments and proliferation of courses within them.

---

[4] Howard Hong, ed., *Integration in the Christian Liberal Arts College* (Northfield, Minn.: St. Olaf College Press, 1956).

The sampling conception of integration in higher education appeals to those who prefer to emphasize concentration in a particular field. The argument is that it is not necessary that the student sample all disciplines to achieve breadth, for each discipline is a sampling of all knowledge and will upon extended contact, ultimately yield breadth as well as depth. It is also possible that the qualities of the teacher and the work habits of the student may be considered as more important than the selection of courses.

The third or relational view is that the various disciplines do have a distinctiveness in content, structure, and method, and are thus relatively independent. Yet, by conscious attention to common or pervasive ideas and concepts which underlie and relate the various fields and by actively seeking for similarities and differences between them, one may identify many unifying concepts and thus clarify what may seem to be inconsistent or contradictory views, methods, and definitions. Furthermore, this relational point of view accepts the possibility that unifying concepts may lead to new course and curricular organizations, and especially to the development of interdisciplinary courses. In this third conception, the instructor has the dual obligation of providing a model of integrative behavior and of motivating the student to engage in such behavior.

A fourth or wholistic view discounts the significance of the divisions of knowledge and argues that they are largely fortuitous. Hence, the individual parts take on meaning only in relationship to other parts in the whole. Unity in this wholistic view may be based upon a highly definitive set of philosophical or religious beliefs. In the extreme it may result in a completely prescribed curriculum with a completely determined pattern of integration provided by philosophical beliefs or religious dogma.

Among university curriculums, the additive and the sampling conceptions of unity are predominant. This is especially true in the arts and sciences, when students are permitted a wide range of choice in the courses taken to satisfy the requirements of breadth and depth. Many of the vocational programs, however, are apparently predicated upon a relational or even a wholistic point of view. The curriculum is planned in relation to an area of work which requires certain knowledge, skills, and ethical standards. The student enrolled in the curriculum also expects that each of the courses which he takes will have some relationship to that goal. Indeed, it is the very attempt of the vocationally oriented student to find such a relationship which often proves most irritating to his professors in the arts and sciences.

In the liberal arts and science colleges, general education and interdisciplinary course offerings are indicative of the attempt to move from the additive or sampling to the relational concept of unity. This attempt is reflected also in concentrations other than departmental majors, comprehensive examinations, and highly individualized education. Some few denominational institutions may achieve the wholistic approach in the common acceptance by faculty and students of a particular religious or philosophical point of view.

Evidences of Effectiveness

Some evidence of the differences in point of view and approach is provided by the criteria set by different groups and individuals for evaluating the effectiveness of a program. Such criteria include the size of the enrollment, the number of degree candidates or majors in the department, the number of candidates who have gone on to study in the graduate school or have been accepted in graduate professional schools, post-graduate employment in good jobs, the satisfaction of the employer, and—occasionally—the satisfaction of the alumnus with his preparation. Occasionally, examination results may be referred to as an evidence of the effectiveness of the program, particularly if some standard examination has been given and the results are highly favorable as compared with those of similar institutions. In relatively few colleges and universities would a long-term assessment of the impact of the educational program on the individual be considered essential. In even fewer would evidence be sought on the social, moral, ethical, and personality development of the individual over the span of the college program. Seldom would any college present as evidence of its effectiveness the percentage of students originally admitted that succeeded in obtaining a degree, although at least one very highly regarded college is reported as priding itself on eliminating 40 per cent of the very select group of freshmen before their sophomore year. The inadequacy of such evidence of effectiveness of colleges must surely be apparent to any thoughtful person.

Accreditation provides one means of overall evaluation of a particular program or institution. Accrediting agencies have rightfully come in for a great deal of criticism in regard to the highly specific, statistical, normative type of evidence upon which they base their judgments. But they have been criticized just as loudly when highly subjective opinions of a school or program have been registered by groups of visiting examiners. The recurrent expressions of interest on the part of accrediting associations and examiners for evidence which would indicate the effectiveness of an institution in bringing about changes in its students have had little result. Such evidence is just not available. Thus accrediting agencies have had to make do with what evidence they could find.

Extracurricular Factors
and the Student Personnel Program

Extracurricular or cocurricular experiences can be as vital and as significant as the more formal classroom and academic experiences in promoting the development of the individual student. The ideal envisaged in some colleges is that residence hall, counseling, student organization, and student activity programs are part of the curriculum of the institution. A realistic view is that much more could be done to relate the various facets of the student experience, but that any attempt to plan every aspect of this experience is ill-advised. Many of the very extensive student personnel programs and planned programs of student activity are an indication of the lack of unity and of challenge in the academic program. If the formal curriculum is only a series of isolated courses, with no challenge beyond completion of routine assignments, students may become busily engaged in finding things to do. Lectures, concerts, and departmental clubs can play a very important educational role, but these programs seldom attract many students, for they are usually not closely related to the formal curriculum and hence only compete with it and other less significant activities for student time. Student government, publications, fraternities, and social activities are inevitably education in some sense, but the experiences therein seldom have much relation to avowed educational goals.

The residence college and the community college or municipal university present entirely different problems in reference to the student personnel program and cocurricular activities. In residence colleges, where a very large percentage of the students is present on the campus, a sizable proportion of the students is likely to be involved in some phase of these cocurricular activities. In the large, municipal university and in the community college, where all students are commuters, the college experience usually reduces itself to class attendance. Many of the students have part-time or even full-time jobs and travel some distance daily between home, school, and job. Adult and other part-time education also exhibit this characteristic. In universities, the cafeteria of profuse offerings repeated every term encourages discontinuous attendance. If the original liberal arts college ideal that a four-year, continuous residence in a college is necessary for a good education, a very large number of unqualified individuals are acquiring the bachelor's degree.

Actually, there is good rationale for arguing that residence is not necessary and that the artificiality of the cocurricular activities in many residence colleges makes them inferior as an educational experience to the pattern in the community college or municipal university where the student relates his academic experiences with world problems because he finds himself moving continually from one to the other. Unity in an educational experience is not achieved by requiring continuous four-year attendance. Furthermore, to insist upon it in the present day would be to bar many individuals from higher education. Even in the four-year residence college, the home-town student and the self-supporting student may restrict their real college experience to the collection of credits.

Perhaps the most effective combination of the academic and the cocurricular is found in institutions where the cocurricular activities have not been set up to compete with the academic but rather have been involved with the academic through a tutorial, preceptor, or house plan with the intellectual effort and relationship between a student and teacher extended into the residence situation rather than separated from it. Other patterns, such as that at Sarah Lawrence, where structured classes have given way to small groups or individual effort, also aid in minimizing the distinction between academic and cocurricular activities. At Antioch College, the cooperative work program, which requires that the student move back and forth between a job and a student role on the campus, is coupled with a cooperative student-faculty approach to facing and resolving institutional problems. This seems to have been rather effective in producing a unified educational experience in which work, study, and experiences which elsewhere might be described as cocurricular, are interrelated in a meaningful way.

Summary of Problems Inherent in Existing Patterns of Organization

The existing patterns of organization in colleges and universities are very great in number and very different from each other. In some institutions, many of the problems of organization have been rather effectively solved. In the modal pattern of organization of colleges and universities, however, a number of the problems of far-reaching implication cannot and will not be solved. Characteristics of this modal structure have already been touched upon:

1. It is a pattern in which a distinction between liberal education and education for a vocation is presumed.

2. The organization of the institutions perpetuates the distinction by setting up departments or colleges of vocational nature and one or more units charged with liberal education.

3. The effective operating unit in the planning of curriculum and instruction is a departmental unit derived either out of its charge of training for a specific vocation or its responsibility for providing instruction in what is regarded as a separate and distinctive discipline or area of knowledge.

4. Faculty members with no grasp of how American higher education has developed, no conception of principles for planning the total curricular experience for an undergraduate, and no concern about the implications of their own decisions with regard to courses and instructional practices on the budget of the institution, nevertheless assume that, if justice were done, they would be in control of the institution and that, at the very least, the determination of the curriculum and of the instructional practices should be their unchallenged domain.

So long as these characteristics persist, there will be a continuation of proliferation of courses and curriculums. The number of possible vocational fields and subvocational fields is continually on the increase, and competition among departments encourages listing of specific curriculums, lest prospective students be attracted elsewhere. Course and curriculum proliferation is accompanied by insufficient attention and emphasis on instruction and academic advising. The goal is to attract students to a department and even to an institution by means of a wide range of courses and curriculums, rather than by quality of instruction and educational planning.

Variations in requirements in college curriculums and among colleges, combined with the cafeteria pattern of course offerings at the various levels, makes sequential planning nearly impossible for all but the minority of students preparing for specific programs in specific colleges. The discounting of rigorous academic admission requirements has some basis in research, but it has also some disadvantages. The able student, who used his freedom of choice in high school to avoid some of the basic disciplines of science, mathematics, or foreign language has thereby lost much of his freedom of choice in college. As more students transfer from the junior college, the problem of disjunction between the first two years and the last two years increases. Junior colleges cannot be expected to offer all the specialized work of the freshman and sophomore years required by various vocational programs offered in the colleges and universities. If, by general agreement, a limited number of basic departmental introductory courses were offered in the freshman and sophomore years, the quality of the work could be considerably improved and the student would be insured of a sequential educational program as he moves from the junior college to the senior college.

The problem of education for women has been much discussed in recent years. The young woman frequently does not want the amount of specialization or concentration involved in the various vocational curriculums or even in the departments of the arts and sciences. She may want to take some courses which will have some value in her expected roles as mother and housewife or as a civic worker. She may also want just enough of vocational training to provide a salable skill for use immediately after graduation and possibly at some later point in life.

Course offerings and curriculum groupings in most colleges are not predicated upon such broad interests. The frustrations engendered from time to time in attempting to work out a reasonable program for a young woman or a young man interested in a broad, liberal education provide evidence of the need for curricular organization and for academic advising and planning which transcend the practices and principles upon which most undergraduate curriculums are presently based.

CHAPTER IV

A New Look at the
Undergraduate Curriculum

It has been noted that the diversity of educational purposes and the autonomy of individual educational institutions make it difficult to paint, except in the broadest of terms, the sequence of developments in higher education in America. Developments visible at a specific time in one or a limited number of institutions may not become widespread for many decades, or they may disappear and reappear later. A reëxamination of the undergraduate curriculum and the development of some new approach to it poses a similar problem. Whatever the problem identified, some institutions will insist that they have already faced and resolved it. And so they may, but most issues recur and the degree of assurance regarding a solution may be inversely related to the adequacy or permanency of that solution. Institutions of higher education have generally muddled through crises with minor modifications or stopgap procedures, rather than by recourse to basic assumptions and principles.

The major purpose of this chapter is to bring together some of the problems and circumstances which command a new approach to undergraduate curriculum development, and to suggest some assumptions which may be useful in replanning the undergraduate program. It is not to be expected that the assumptions or the principles emerging from them will meet with unanimous acceptance. Their purpose will be equally well served if those who object are moved to propose alternatives which will likewise bring under reasoned control the present unsystematic and wildly expanding curriculums.

Among the circumstances which require a reëxamination of the undergraduate curriculum, the need for bridging the gap between liberal and professional or occupational curriculums is predominant. There are those who feel that undergraduate degrees might

59

reasonably become as specialized as graduate degrees, and that common educational elements, common objectives, or a set of principles providing some sense of unity in the undergraduate program are not really required. But, even if it be assumed that a Bachelor of Engineering or of Business is entirely distinct from a Bachelor of Arts, there remains the necessity for these professional and technical curriculums to include some work from the arts and sciences simply because the concepts, ideas, and methodology are necessary in the development of the particular vocational field. Therefore, a problem of appropriate relationship and balance clearly exists. In suggesting this as a major circumstance which requires a new approach, the assumption is made that there will be no return to a general requirement of a four-year nonpreparatory liberal arts degree program as the general and immediate post-secondary school higher education experience, for the mores of modern culture emphasize the importance of education in reference to productive employment.

A careful examination of the nature of liberal and professional curriculums suggests many ways in which the gap between the two can be bridged. There is much similarity between vocational and liberal objectives. Liberal education emphasizes broad knowledge of the cultural heritage, the ability to think critically and to make wise judgments, and some awareness of the methodologies of the major disciplines. Liberal education also assumes the ability to communicate one's ideas to others and to receive ideas from others. Finally, a liberal education, without assuming an indoctrination in a specific set of values, involves the expectation that an individual will attain an effective set of personal values consistent with liberal tradition. In these broad terms, vocational and liberal objectives are not essentially different.

Professional and technical curriculums also require a body of knowledge necessarily selected in relation to the needs of the field, but not necessarily unrelated to or inconsistent with liberal education goals. The manner in which knowledge is acquired and the way in which it is used is at least as important as the bases for its selection. As vocational curriculums move out of the how-to-do-it initial stage to the development of broad principles and concepts and the ability to apply these, critical thinking, decision-making, and judgment will become prime objectives. In every professional or technical field the ability to communicate with others (whether colleagues or the clients) is essential. Finally, in any professional field, there exists, implicitly or explicitly, a set of ethical considerations which describe or delimit the way in which the competent and honorable person in the field operates. By contributing to the objectives of critical thinking, communication, and value orientation, thoughtful and inspired teaching in the vocational field may have every bit as much liberal education impact as teaching in more traditional nonvocational fields.

To accomplish this more fully, planners of vocational and technical curriculums may shift from emphasizing specific problems, prescriptions, and skills to stressing the assimilation of a fund of knowledge, principles, and concepts by recourse to which the individual may himself make judgments as to how a problem should be resolved. The engineering college faculty should not encourage the engineering student to expect that each little educational experience will be immediately identifiable in relationship to a task in the engineering field. No one can predict with assurance just what principles or skills will be most significant in the next ten or twenty years. Education based on current practice may produce students who lack both the means and the incentive to engage in creative or original thinking. Professional and technical work should be so selected and taught as to be in accord with the liberal tradition and contribute to a student's liberal education. That which does not should be screened out and assigned to the trade or technical school.

Another circumstance which requires a new look at the undergraduate curriculum is the continuing proliferation of courses and curriculums. Although increasing budgets and increasing difficulty in balancing them act somewhat as a brake, financial considerations slow up the rate of proliferation. Course proliferation is of too many types to be readily controlled; it may even be difficult to identify. The following types are frequently noted:

1. Slight variations in course content to satisfy the whims of other departments. An elementary course may be given an advanced number to provide credit for the upperclassman or graduate student.

2. Slight variations in content coverage and in credit hours to provide for curriculums in which 3 credits but not 4 can be given to study of a particular area.

3. Slight variations in prerequisites of several courses in the same department to accommodate students with differing backgrounds; for example, physics based on knowledge of calculus, physics based on knowledge of algebra and trigonometry, physics requiring no mathematics.

4. Duplicating and overlapping courses in different departments. These may arise out of any of the three points above or from attempts to establish squatter's rights in new territory; *e.g.,* social psychology and psychology of social groups.

5. Courses which are unduly narrow and specialized at the undergraduate level and more appropriate for the graduate school.

6. Courses which are unduly elementary or entirely inappropriate for the college level; *e.g.,* plumbing, house and barn wiring.

Careful definition of the essential areas of knowledge upon which a group of related vocational fields and specializations could be based, and the selection of a limited number of basic courses which would provide the student with maximal power and flexibility as he moves into one of these broad groups, should help to eliminate these many offerings with their petty differences and their atomization of the curriculum.

The third reason for reëxamining the educational program is the incentive to and impact on student learning. Programs which spread students thinly over a large number of courses force students to engage in many preparations and discourage them from lingering upon significant ideas or from taking responsibility for pursuing their education beyond the day-by-day requirements. Such programs also impose an unnecessary burden of scheduled class hours and different preparations upon staff members. As newer media— including automated teaching—are adapted to educational programs, it may be possible to provide a better quality of education —even to larger groups of students. Attention to the improvement of instruction has been sporadic and generally halfhearted, because the focus has always been on what the teacher does. By some fantastic stretch of the concept of academic freedom, it has also been argued—although not in quite these words—that the teacher should be free to do as poor a job of teaching as he wishes. His actions are not subject to review and improvement; thus improvement of instruction becomes a subject for conferences but not a cause for action. If the teacher is viewed as an instrument to encourage learning on the part of students, it becomes apparent that his role in planning a set of experiences assumes more importance than his presence in a classroom.

As a fourth circumstance requiring a new look at the undergraduate curriculum, it may be suggested that the departmental, divisional, and other organizational features of the undergraduate college often interfere with rather than promote good education. The department built around a discipline has provided a pleasant home for the specialist, and has probably been effective in promoting intellectual exchanges which have facilitated scholarly activity and research. But the department, as the primary unit in the college and university, has also tended to detach the attention of the faculty members from the problems of the institution as a whole, and has made them disinterested in advising students on matters other than selection of courses in their own department. The difficulties found in the universities in staffing interdisciplinary projects, and the emergence of a variety of institutes, bureaus, centers, and the like demonstrate that there is some question as to the general efficacy of the existing departmental organization not only in promoting undergraduate education, but also in promoting frontier research of the interdisciplinary type.

The preoccupation of most of the present undergraduate programs with Western culture constitutes a fifth circumstance calling for reëxamination of the curriculum. There is a need for persons to have some understanding of other cultures—especially of those now competing with America for precedence in the world. Our own cultural heritage must be reëxamined to see whether it includes more elements of non-Western culture than have been recognized, and to determine whether these and other elements may be introduced into curriculums in order to provide an international outlook as well as better understanding of American culture itself. The value-concerns of liberal education can be achieved only if the undergraduate is brought face to face with value-systems of cultures which are in marked contrast with his own.

A sixth circumstance for a reëxamination of the curriculum is the possible disjunction between the demands of undergraduate instruction and those of the graduate school which provides the preparation of the college teacher. It is strange that college teaching is perhaps the one occupation which presumes to identify itself as a profession and yet provides no specific professional preparation. Yet the new college instructor is expected to know something about how to organize courses, read students' papers, prepare examinations, conduct a seminar, and encourage students to engage in independent study. If graduate schools had restricted themselves to degrees solely concerned with advanced study and research in traditional disciplines, the deficiencies of doctoral programs would be less obvious. But since the planning of graduate curriculums and the expansion of graduate degrees have been in the direction of making specific adjustment for other vocational fields, there should be a similar adjustment for the field of college teaching.

Bridging the Gap Between Liberal and Professional Curriculums

By pursuing systematically the similarities in objectives of professional and of liberal education, by redefining and reducing the offerings and sequences in the basic science and arts disciplines, and by eliminating the "how-to-do-it" or techniques courses of the vocational curriculums, professional and technical offerings can become more liberal. Some of the not-so-liberal arts and science offerings might also become more liberal.

There is also need for some plan or model whereby vocational curriculums can be redefined and regrouped in order to bring related vocational fields into a more productive relationship and to establish a sequential relationship to those disciplines of the arts and sciences upon which the vocational fields are based. For instance nursing, medicine, medical technology, veterinary medicine, and dietetics are often widely separated in the university. Nursing and medical technology may be affiliated with the arts and sciences college, may be attached to some other college, or exist as independent or quasi-independent schools. Dietetics is frequently a part of a college of home economics. Veterinary medicine and human medicine usually exist as independent colleges or schools. These vocations share many common concerns and require some common background of knowledge. Surely some association of these curriculums and of the faculties involved could result in mutual gain to the respective fields by use of carefully planned fundamental courses and possibly by the elimination of unnecessarily specialized courses. Social work has much in common with counseling, special education, and even with teaching, but usually exists as an independent graduate school. Could there be mutual gain from grouping together a number of those curriculums which are essentially applications of the social sciences?

Colleges of home economics present a somewhat different problem. Included therein are several curriculums which have little in common except an elusive concern for the home and family. Courses in nutrition and dietetics are largely based on the sciences. Courses in home management and child development are largely dependent upon psychology and the social sciences. Courses in clothing and textiles, depending upon the emphasis, may be either applied arts or dependent upon the physical sciences. Home economics education also attempts to turn out secondary school home economics teachers equipped to teach in all these areas. The low quality of high school home economics instruction may be caused, in part, by the virtual impossibility of educating one individual adequately in what have become essentially separate specialties. It should be noted further that home economists are usually women, and are seldom interested in physics and engineering. Hence, house architecture, design of household equipment, home heating, and the like—although problems of the home and family—are not usually dealt with effectively by the home economist. The question which may then be legitimately raised is whether the various subspecialties loosely grouped in home economics might not gain by being regrouped with other curriculums. Psychologists, sociologists, social workers, and educators are frequently as much concerned with problems in the home and family area as home economists are. Architects, engineers, landscape architects, and others can contribute to house planning and household equipment. After such regrouping, it might become desirable or necessary to organize interdisciplinary teams to deal with pervasive problems of the home and family at some new and higher level than is possible at present.

There are other areas in which similar questions arise. Is there really much basis for the extensive distinctions between curriculums for chemistry and for chemical engineering? In at least one major chemical plant, the initial job assignments for both fields are much the same. Might not the undergraduate engineer profitably spend more time in mathematics and basic sciences? Apparently Massachusetts Institute of Technology, California Institute of Technology, and some other first-class engineering schools think so. In such schools, increased emphasis has also been placed on the social science and humanistic studies. Colleges of agriculture, faced with falling enrollments and the disinterest of graduates in farming, have tended in recent years to develop programs in agricultural business and in agricultural science. The first is in direct competition with business administration curriculums, and the latter is and should be more a major in science than in agriculture.

It may be, then, that the various undergraduate and graduate professional and technical fields could be more meaningfully defined and regrouped in relation to the basic areas of knowledge upon which they draw. Figure 2, although it has many apparent

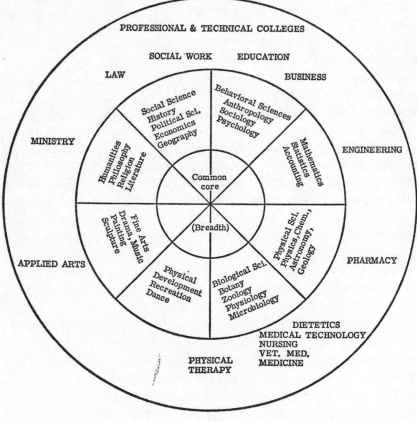

Figure 2

limitations, suggests a possible pattern which might emerge. For all undergraduates there might be some common general education requirements embracing the major fields of knowledge. Students would then move to a level of relatively broad specialization in the sciences, social sciences, humanities, or arts and then into professional or technical courses built upon these. Much of the specialization of the vocational undergraduate curriculums would then be deferred to on-the-job experience or to the graduate level. The student would, however, have a much better basic preparation for maintaining pace with the rapidly changing requirements of technological society.

Implications

For course organization. If such a model were adopted, the courses offered in the various arts and science departments would need to be planned so as to develop broad understandings of essential facts, principles, and concepts and also to provide a wide range of problem situations in which the student could develop some power in applying his knowledge in their solution. These problems should sample those of the various fields into which the students would later go. Thus the professional and technical faculties would be expected to contribute to the planning of these courses and perhaps occasionally to engage in teaching them. The science faculty, for example, would no longer embrace only those courses in the "pure" sciences but would include all those operating in the applied sciences. Courses heavily slanted toward particular vocational fields would be abandoned in favor of courses developing ideas broadly applicable in a group of related fields.

Conceivably, in many cases, departmental courses would be replaced by broader interdisciplinary offerings. An interdisciplinary sequence of courses in the biological sciences, for example, might, after careful consideration of the needs of all students and dependent vocational fields, be found superior to the departmental type of offerings now prevalent. Whereas most universities offer beginning genetics in a number of different guises, a single offering might be found to provide better grounding for all students. In some subjects, such as statistics, a sequence of introductory courses might require an organization in which a portion of the instruction would be supplied by the faculty in each of several areas. Thus students of business, after being exposed to general principles along with other students, might meet in several sessions with professors from the college of business who would engage the students in application of these principles to the problems peculiar to business. Alternatively, such intensive applications might be deferred to advanced courses offered in the professional college.

Such restructuring would require abandonment of the usual departmental autonomy in course planning; determination of course content, course sequence, and instructional practices would be institution-wide. But it is the best education for the student rather than the convenience of the faculty that should be the dominating consideration.

For the graduate schools. There are some obvious implications for the graduate schools. On one hand, increased association among the several graduate programs drawing upon the same bodies of knowledge might improve the quality of the several programs. For example, social work might benefit from closer relationship to advanced study in counseling, in psychology, and in sociology. Such a reorganization might also permit graduate training to be viewed in clearer perspective in relationship to the relevant undergraduate study upon which it is based. Students, too, might see their undergraduate program as leading naturally into any one of several related graduate specialties.

Graduate training in the arts and sciences might also come to be viewed, in some areas, as less necessarily departmental. But even if departmentalization were still viewed as essential at the graduate level, it is not necessarily so at the undergraduate level.

Summary

It has been suggested that undergraduate specialization has proceeded too far—too far to provide some modicum of a liberal outlook in the graduates and too far to enable the graduates to adjust to the rapidly changing nature of the specialties which they enter. The knowledge required in the several vocations for which colleges may justifiably provide an education exceeds that which any student can reasonably acquire in four years. The particular knowledge and skill which a practitioner may require in a narrow field today may not be required a year from now. It is far more important that he have the basic knowledge and abilities to keep abreast of his field to adapt to new developments and new requirements within it. Properly construed, then, undergraduate vocational preparation should be sequentially planned in relationship to the basic areas of knowledge upon which the vocation is based. The major in engineering or in mathematics or in physics would differ primarily in the courses taken in the last two years, and these courses, in turn, would differ primarily in the nature of the problems confronted rather than in the nature of the principles and ideas employed. This is what is suggested by the following succinct statement as to the purposes of undergraduate education made by John A. Hannah, President of Michigan State University: [1]

> In the final analysis, we believe that an educated man in a democracy is one who is trained and conditioned to be an effective citizen. He need not necessarily be a man who has attained great wealth, or professional distinction, or high public office. He may not be known far beyond the borders of his own community.
> But he will have been educated to contribute to society *economically* to the limits of his creative and productive skills.
> He will have been educated to contribute *socially* by his understanding of the world around him and his tolerance for the rights and opinions of others.
> He will have been educated to contribute *morally* by his acceptance and observance of the fundamental values.
> And he will have been educated to contribute *politically* by his reasoned, thinking approach to political issues, his rejection of demogogic appeals, and his willingness and ability to lead or to follow with equal intelligence.
> With such definitions of education in mind, we do not think so much of graduating engineers or chemists or teachers or home economists or agriculturalists or businessmen as of graduating educated men and women trained to be effective citizens of our democracy —men and women ready and willing to assume the duties of leadership in a nation crying for intelligent direction and guidance in a world full of confusion and insecurity and doubt.

This view suggests that undergraduate programs are not to be designed to prepare specialists, but rather to educate men and women

---

[1] John A. Hannah, *Michigan State University Catalog,* 1960–61 (East Lansing, Mich.), p. 7.

for their roles as individuals, parents, workers, and citizens in a democratic society. Such a goal can neither be defined nor insured by inflexible curricular requirements. Arbitrary distinctions between general and vocational education hinder rather than aid the development of educational programs consonant with this broad conception of the educated graduate.

Higher education then should be designed to help the student increase his knowledge and improve his basic skills, but it should place greater emphasis on developing systematic modes of thought and evaluation. Thus higher education prepares the student to lead a more satisfying and productive life as a citizen, and provides concurrently, if not simultaneously, a background or foundation for a vocation or for further professional or graduate training. These two functions of higher education are not clearly separable.

Nor is higher education entirely separable from preceding levels of education. Indeed, it should not be; rather, it should be a continuation, sequential rather than repetitious in nature. It is therefore necessary that the student's higher education experience differ in nature, as well as in content, from his earlier education. Elementary and secondary education should be primarily concerned with promoting the acquisition of basic facts and skills. Higher education should place primary emphasis on introducing the student to: (1) unifying ideas, concepts, principles, and methods; (2) primary rather than secondary sources; (3) a critical, sophisticated, and value-conscious approach to issues and problems. By designing college courses and curriculums in reference to these considerations, the knowledge and skills acquired in high school can be used as a foundation for an education at once more analytical and more integrative than previously experienced. The accomplishment of this goal may also require redefinition of secondary school preparation in relation to various college programs and the introduction of a testing program to insure the adequacy of secondary school preparation.

The quality of any undergraduate program depends not only on the courses and curriculum requirements, but as much—and perhaps more—on the instruction and the advising provided by the faculty and on the presence of an elusive but nevertheless tangible atmosphere or environment favorable to learning. The "tone" or "press" of an institution provides the incentive or motivation which

encourages the individual to accept some obligation for and take
some initiative in self-education. However good the faculty and
other resources, all meaningful learning is, after all, an individual
and deeply personal experience. The fostering of the incentive for
and the development of the means to continue self-education
constitute the most important values of an undergraduate program,
for they are essential to continuing the intellectual and moral
growth of each graduate.

It has already been suggested that rigidly defined curriculums
deprive the student and his advisers of the opportunity of thinking
through the significance of the undergraduate program, of laying
individual plans for such a program, and of seeing it take form in
course sequences and other less formal educational experiences
within the university. If a rigidly defined curriculum is found un-
satisfactory, it does not follow that complete freedom—either for
the faculty or for the students—is desirable. Some broad concepts
and principles with regard to the undergraduate program are
necessary.

Any set of principles, however, either constitutes or is based
upon a set of assumptions and it is well that these assumptions be
explicitly set down—at least to whatever extent they are identifiable.
Some assumptions or convictions are implied if not fully expressed
in the statement by John Hannah regarding undergraduate education. An individual, to fulfill the many roles he has in society, needs
some breadth of knowledge. He needs also some similarity of
experience and of knowledge with his associates, and he requires a
high degree of mastery of communication skills so that he may
exchange ideas with his associates and resolve issues as they arise.
The individual also needs some depth, which may be encouraged
by a departmental major, a more broadly or narrowly conceived
concentration, or by a vocational specialty. The element of depth
provides sufficient grasp of some discipline or area of performance
so that the student may begin to act independently and make his
own decisions within this area. Depth—however defined—will
ordinarily involve vocational as well as purely educational experience. These assumptions of recognitions of need are inadequate to
provide a really new look at the undergraduate program; they must
give way to the more explicit assumptions below. These assumptions arise out of the analysis which has already been made of the

problems of the undergraduate curriculums. Some have previously been stated or implied.

Assumptions

1. The role of undergraduate higher education, both in relation to the secondary school and the community college which it follows and in relation to graduate education and vocational activity which it precedes and for which it prepares, requires clarification in regard to objectives, subject matter sequences, and specificity of preparation.

2. In a society characterized by a rapidly developing technology, many individuals will be faced with the necessity of continuing education or of complete re-education in order to enter into new fields or keep abreast of new developments in their own. Undergraduate education should prepare individuals for this contingency.

3. With the range of vocations continually increasing, students entering college will find it increasingly difficult to make highly specific vocational choices. Indecision and alteration of initial decisions will become increasingly common. Curriculums should be built with a flexibility which will permit reasonable changes in career plans during as well as following the college years.

4. All courses and curriculums offered in a college or university should be based on a defined substantive body of knowledge, concepts, and principles selected from the basic disciplines of the arts and sciences. By extension of the scope of this basic body of knowledge, and by increased emphasis on the problem-solving process employing this basic knowledge, technical and professional education programs can increase the flexibility and power of their graduates.

5. In the next several decades, colleges will admit more and better qualified students than ever before, but neither the funds nor the qualified personnel will be available to maintain the present faculty-student ratio.

6. Faculty salaries and time for research and scholarly activity should be materially increased in the next few years. This is especially true of the university, but liberal arts and even community college faculties should have some individuals whose efforts are devoted to synthesizing new developments and relating them to the undergraduate curriculum. But these goals can be accomplished only if instructional productivity is markedly increased.

7. There is no direct or simple relationship between educational expenditure per student and the quality of education supplied; it is therefore possible to seek simultaneously for increased efficiency and higher quality.

8. Since the curricular and course offerings and instructional practices of any department or college require a commitment of

limited resources which affects all other units, the offerings, instructional practices and plans of any one department or college must be subject to review and modification in order to insure optimum usage of the total resources.

9. Although the responsibility for the quality and characteristics of graduate programs, because of their specialized nature, must rest primarily in the departments and colleges, the responsibility for definition and approval of undergraduate curriculums and courses rests with the entire institution. This is especially true for those courses in the sciences and arts which serve a large student clientele from other colleges, departments, and curriculums.

10. In order to achieve an institution-wide point of view regarding undergraduate curriculums, it is necessary that administrative officers exercise strong leadership in policy development and in the interpretation to the faculty of these policies and the reasons underlying them.

11. In an institution which is part of a centrally supported system (public or private) of higher education, program development cannot proceed independently of what is done in other universities and colleges of the system. Hence, the board of trustees, acting with and upon the advice of the top administrative officers, has special responsibility in reviewing existing educational programs and proposals for the development of new ones, in reference to the needs of the supporting clientele and the programs of other educational institutions in the system.

12. Although an institution must always be sensitive to the requests and demands of students and citizen groups for the offering of services, courses, and curriculums, the institution itself must finally be the judge of the appropriateness of any program to its purposes and its resources. This judgment can be rendered wisely only if a clear set of principles exists upon which it can be based.

13. Students should accept more responsibility for planning and for proceeding independently with their own learning.

14. Courses should be grouped into larger blocks of subject matter and there should be an associated decrease in scheduled class hours as students progress in assuming responsibility for their own learning.

15. Teaching and learning resources should be closely coordinated with a view to defining more precisely the role of faculty members, assistants, aides, and students.

16. New materials, aids, and methods should be developed to facilitate higher levels of student learning and to stimulate research on the learning process.

17. Physical and organizational arrangements should be so planned as to foster learning and encourage independent study.

18. The number, function, location, and architecture of new

facilities should be planned so as to foster the learning process and group students and faculty for effectiveness, relationships, and efficiency in physical movement and maintenance.

19. Administrative, planning, and budgetary procedures should be so designed and carried out as to enforce acceptance of these assumptions.

CHAPTER V

Principles for the Development
of the Undergraduate Curriculum

A college in a university should not be just an administrative convenience made up of a congeries of unrelated, quasi-independent schools, departments, and curriculums; rather, it should result from a grouping of faculty members and of fields of study which have some common elements. These common elements may be found in the similarity in the tasks in which the graduates of the several curriculums of the college engage, or in the mutual dependence of these several curriculums upon the several disciplines which are included in the college. If a college possesses some elements of such unity, then it may be expected that every student and every curriculum within that college will have a core of common educational experiences inclusive of the elements which make up the related specialties of a single professional field. Thus a college of engineering might find certain historical or philosophical considerations, as well as analytical and methodological considerations, appropriate to a common educational experience for all engineers. Since all professional and technical programs also draw heavily on one or more of the basic disciplines encompassed within the college of science and arts, it is to be anticipated that every professional and technical college will have a significant requirement of common courses from the college of science and arts.

A department in a college should not be simply an administrative unit offering a wide array of unrelated courses. Rather, it should embrace a single discipline or field of study and offer a single major to undergraduate students with a large proportion of the courses being a common requirement for all majors in the department.[1] The department may also offer a limited number of elective advanced

---

[1] Rigorous application of this principle would require that each foreign language would be offered by a separate department. This is not intended, but it is intended that there be but one major in each foreign language—rather than several, each emphasizing literature of different periods, for example.

courses giving some intimation of the various specialties to which this discipline has given birth. Thus, the department, while providing a home for faculty members whose interests may be highly specialized in subfields of the basic discipline, preserves its identity and unity by offering basic undergraduate courses which define the common foundation of these specialties. Not all curriculums entail departmental majors or represent applications of single disciplines. Special curriculums may be organized which draw upon or require knowledge and experience from a number of different departments or even colleges. In such cases, the designation of school rather than department may give appropriate recognition to the nature of the curriculum.

In the broadest sense, the curriculum includes all the course offerings and other experiences which have relevance to the student's attainment of academic goals. In a more restricted sense, a curriculum—especially when modified by adjectives or phrases such as "liberal arts" or "management and merchandising"—refers to a more or less rigidly defined pattern of courses. The bases for the specification of the courses may be found in principles defining a liberal education or in an analysis of the requirements for specialized vocational fields.

Depth. It is not inappropriate to regard undergraduate professional or technical education as offering the equivalent of the liberal arts major requirement. It has already been noted that one may define in a professional field certain general requirements pertaining to all students in that field, and certain special requirements pertaining to subdivisions of the field. This is quite analogous to the common and specialized elements making up a departmental major. The concept of depth starts from the assumption that every professional or technical field is essentially an application of one or more of the disciplines comprehended within the liberal arts and sciences. Each field can therefore provide an experience in depth not essentially different from that provided by advanced courses in the departments of the arts, literature, and sciences, and a liberal education experience in no way inferior to them.

Breadth. Three different, although evidently interrelated, conceptions of breadth have been identified (see Chapter II). One is the student's contact with the major divisions of knowledge. A second is the student's contact with different systems of value and with different cultures as a basis for reflection upon and critical examination of his own values and those of his own culture. A third is the student's contact with the distinctive methodology of the various disciplines.

The liberal arts requirements of vocational programs are sometimes viewed as recognition of the breadth component, but breadth may also be supplied by vocational courses. The common core requirement for a group of related or technical specialties may readily include elements of history, ethics, philosophy, and methodology, which contribute to breadth. An example is a course having as its theme the impact of technology on American culture. This has been required in at least one undergraduate engineering program and suggests that science and arts majors might gain in breadth by electing such vocational offerings.

Prerequisites and sequences. Prerequisites and sequences are closely related, for course sequences are meaningless unless prerequisites for subsequent courses are established. Without prerequisites and some tangible concept of sequence, the concept of depth itself is largely lost. Prerequisites, however, should not be rigidly defined in terms of courses and credits. Rather, the knowledge and competencies involved should be so defined that an individual who has acquired them can be recognized and admitted to any course for which he is qualified.

The concept of sequence has meaning in relationship to breadth, as well as to depth. Breadth and depth are always complementary and relative. The chemical engineer must know some physics and mathematics and have some conception of economics. He must know something about engineering generally as well as chemical engineering specially. Thus specialization must always have elements of breadth, occurring at various levels and having various degrees of immediate relevance to any specific problem. Indeed the genius of a professional or technical specialty which requires collegiate level education is that it synthesizes knowledge from several fields and derives ways to use this knowledge in the solution of problems which transcend the bounds of the increasingly narrow disciplines.

Integration. Integration is not something which is ever fully achieved. It is, rather, a state of mind required for both students and instructors. When a new chemical compound with therapeutic potentialities is discovered, the task of relating this development to existing knowledge is different for different persons. The chemist is interested in how the substance is related to other substances in structure and in chemical properties; the physician is concerned with fitting this drug into his existing array of therapeutic agents; and the chemical engineer may be primarily concerned with developing an economical manufacturing process by applying knowledge gained from past experiences with similar compounds. Each individual faces a different integrative task because each has a different background and different concerns.

It is doubtful that any attempt to achieve integrative educational experiences can be successful except as students have some significant common area of experience. If students and faculty do share a considerable segment of experience, then it becomes possible to work together in advanced courses in an attempt to interrelate the acquired knowledge of the student, and to apply this knowledge to some of the problems and issues in the world around him. It has sometimes been noted in follow-up studies of college and university graduates that they are unable to relate the college experience directly to the problems faced in their roles as workers and citizens after leaving college. This inability is an index of the extent to which instruction in the college and university has failed to help the student perceive interrelationships between his learning experiences and the world.

Many institutions have found a senior integrative seminar particularly useful at this point because it poses the possibility of examining the total impact and significance of the previous years of college experience, and then looking ahead to consider the relevance of that knowledge and experience to some of the current issues which will be faced upon graduation. But the experience of numerous colleges suggests that unless previous attempts have been made to cultivate this point of view, the seminar itself will fail— first, because the students are incapable of developing integrative points of view in such a limited span of time and, second, because the very absence of prior experience suggests that the faculty themselves are unable to lead such a seminar.

Course load. It is not always recognized that the load of the faculty and of the students depends greatly on the number of courses for which the individual is responsible at a given time. The faculty member responsible for four or five different courses may find no time to prepare in depth for a single one of them. Similarly, the student who is forced to run from one to another of five, six, or even seven courses, never really immerses himself in any one of them. He contents himself with meeting the minimum requirements. To the extent that courses can be grouped into fewer and larger units and be assigned larger blocks of time, both student and faculty can achieve both greater depth and greater breadth. The significant ideas of many formerly discrete courses will appear but in a more interrelated and hence more meaningful way. It is also desirable to strive for the definition of blocks of educational experience which transcend the single courses. To the extent that an individual student may perceive his education as taking shape over a span of months or even years rather than on a day-to-day basis, he may take responsibility for and provide self-direction in forwarding his education.

Objectives. Objectives should be stated which make evident to the student what he is expected to achieve by his educational experience. Naturally, these objectives will vary somewhat for various areas of that experience, but to the extent that the objectives can provide direction over a group of courses rather than degenerate into statements of particular factual knowledge and skills related to a single course, college experience will assume a greater unity. Having accepted such objectives, the student may look at the kinds of assignments and educational experiences laid out for him more critically than ever, to determine whether these are really relevant for him in the achievement of the stated objectives. In some cases they may not be, and at this point the student and his adviser may plan an alternative, such as credit by examination or substitution of another course or experience.

Finally, some note should be taken of the qualities of the experience. The most apparent attempt to date on the part of colleges to consider the characteristics of particular experiences is found in the science laboratory. In effect, the objective is that the student have a certain kind of experience with the gadgetry of science, although to be sure the intent is also that he perceive something of the nature of scientific experimentation as a means to new knowledge. The freshman composition course is another example of a requirement in which heavy emphasis is placed on a particular type of experience. These two examples suggest that it is desirable to have several courses which require extensive writing experience, several which involve some oral activity, and others which involve significant group discussions, case method type of instruction, and so on. Each of these particular types of experiences has, altogether apart from the content involved, an educational significance just as great as that of a laboratory requirement. Some means should be found to assure that each student has such experiences. It may also be appropriate to insist that the student have some contact with history, philosophy, and religion, which represent approaches to knowledge, as well as with humanities, social science, and science, which represent areas of knowledge.

A Curriculum model. The pattern exhibited in Table 1 suggests a possible organization of the undergraduate program, in which arts and science majors and professional and technical under-graduate school majors can be viewed in much the same way. This curriculum model involves six components, each of which is in evidence in both types of curriculums. The university-wide core (A), suggested arbitrarily as 25 per cent of the degree requirements, applies to all students. If the professional or technical school degree requirements exceed the usual 120 credits in academic courses, the core percentage would drop correspondingly. These courses would not necessarily be identical for all students, provided that other grounds than content are found for defining the significance of this common core. In liberal arts colleges, which offer several vocational specialties, component A might be the basic requirement for all degrees, or components A and B might be merged to insure that 55 per cent of the student's work is in liberal studies.

The general requirement in arts and sciences B, suggested as 30 per cent of the degree requirements, would provide additional liberal education requirements in language and mathematics. For arts and science majors this element might be merged with C, the division-wide specialization core, which is expected to provide some common experiences and understandings in the divisional area. This requirement should provide some undergirding for the major and in that respect is the beginning of specialization. From another angle, the divisional requirement is a breadth requirement which helps relate the departmental majors to closely associated disciplines.

For the professional or technical school component, B provides the undergirding upon which the field is based. It is expected that this component would be essentially a common one for all students in a given college. If it is impossible to agree on such common bases, some doubt is cast on the rationale for the association of the several specialties into a single college. For the professional or

TABLE 1

A CURRICULUM MODEL *

	Curriculum Component	Per Cent of Degree Requirements (Based on 120 Semester Credits)	Arts and Science Majors	Technical & Professional
A.	University-wide Core	25	Basic courses in Composition, Social Science, Science, Humanities	
B.	General Requirement in Arts & Science	30	Foreign Languages, Mathematics, Additional breadth	Concentration in the disciplines upon which field is based
C.	College or Divisional-wide Specialization Core	10	Divisional requirements to buttress majors	Common requirement for all specialties included in a college
D.	Major or Concentration Common Requirement	15	Departmental core required of all majors in a dept.	Common requirement within each of the several specialties included in a college
E.	Major or Concentration Electives	10	Elective within major field	Electives within specialty
F.	Free Electives	10	Preferably not to be taken in dept. of major	Preferably not to be taken in professional or technical college

* The percentages presented in this model are arbitrary, but analysis of a number of undergraduate curriculums indicates that they are reasonable. Physical education and other nonacademic requirements are ignored in setting up this model.

technical college, component C may comprehend historical, philosophical, and ethical materials and a few other general professional courses of wide applicability. Thus Consumer Economics might be deemed relevant to all home economics specialties. Unless all the curriculums of a technical or professional college accept such a common core, component C becomes meaningless, and the grouping of curriculums again comes into question.

Component D, approximately 15 per cent of the degree requirements and perhaps as much as 60 per cent of the usual departmental major, makes explicit the view that all departmental majors should have numerous courses or experiences in common and that an analogous pattern should hold for vocational specialties. Component E, approximately 10 per cent, is suggested as elective within the major. This may actually be left to student choice, or several undergraduate curriculums with minor variations in course requirement may be outlined to attract students and to inform the public and prospective employers of the relevancy of the departmental major to these fields. Finally, component F suggests that every student should have some free electives. No curriculum should be so planned as to specify student selection of these free electives to complete the program. Preferably, the student should not use these electives in the immediate department or area of specialization, but formulization of this preference would destroy the freedom of election. Just as surely, narrow vocationally-oriented advising would also destroy that freedom.

Although percentages of degree requirements and therefore credits have been specified in this model, specific credit requirements will not resolve the problems. The essential considerations lie in the continuing interplay of breadth and depth, in the development of a sequential pattern in which advanced study is based on prerequisite study, and in a much larger element of common learning experiences which will aid in developing sequence and force the elimination of a large number of courses which have led to an unmanageable curriculum and to expensive education.

Principles for Curriculum Planning

This section makes explicit as principles some of the ideas developed in the preceding sections and adds others necessary to the development of an effective and economical undergraduate program. The principles pertain specifically to a university structure, but with minor modifications they are also applicable to the curriculums of liberal arts colleges.

General principles

1. All curriculums should start with a 25 per cent college-wide or university-wide core or general education requirement. It is not necessary that the core be defined by a few courses required of all students, but it is necessary that the courses be planned for breadth and be equally suitable for all students.

2. All curriculums should require an additional 30 per cent of the initial 120 credit hours in courses generally accepted as included in the liberal arts and sciences, although these courses may not always be located in the college of arts and sciences.

3. All curriculums in a single vocational college should include a common group of courses adding up to at least 10 per cent of the total requirement.

4. Each major or curriculum should also specify a common depth or specialization requirement of 15 per cent of the degree requirement or approximately three-fifths of the credit requirements for a departmental major.

5. Approximately 10 per cent of the initial 120 credit hours should be reserved for an elective major component or for specialization directed toward sub-vocations in the general field for which a college curriculum is regarded as preparatory.

6. All curriculums should leave uncommitted at least 12 credits (10 per cent) for electives to be chosen by the student and his adviser.

7. All curriculums should be carefully screened to insure that the goals are reasonably attainable in a four-year program (or other specified period) and that the courses and other educational experiences required for this attainment are appropriate in the college or university.

8. Any credit course should either develop or utilize a definable substantive body of content. Skills of a repetitive, how-to-do-it nature should be minimized as course objectives, and relegated to the laboratory, to field experience, or simply specified as required

demonstrable levels of competency for acceptance, continuation, or graduation in the field.

9. Each department should offer only one major (although there must be obvious exceptions, as in foreign languages). A few courses at the junior or senior year may be oriented to sub-specialties, but otherwise specialization should be at the post-graduate level.

10. Departmental specialization beyond the common requirement should be in courses offered at the junior and senior levels and developed on the assumption that the common requirements are either prerequisites or taken concurrently.

11. Special courses or sections for majors in other fields should be resisted, unless the need for them can be demonstrated to be more fundamental than a matter of one or two credits or a slightly different selection or organization of content materials.

12. Introductory course offerings in the basic arts and sciences should be developed in relation to the needs of the total college or university rather than on narrow, specialized departmental concerns. Only thus, is it possible to insist that each technical or professional curriculum use these basic courses in preference to developing its own.

13. With possibly a few exceptions, courses should be planned on a 4- or 5-credit basis and with the exception that class sessions, especially in courses beyond the freshman year, may be less than the number of credits.[2]

14. Laboratory requirements in all courses should be reduced to a minimum by carefully defining the objectives to be met and by providing the means whereby the student achievement of these objectives can be determined.

15. Departments in areas attractive as general electives may appropriately offer an advanced course or two at the junior or senior level without prerequisites other than the relevant courses of the general core requirement. Since these courses would not fall into the sequential course organization of the departments, it is

---

[2] If the 4- or 5-credit course pattern were adopted, requirements could more appropriately be phrased in reference to courses rather than credits. The 4-credit pattern is sometimes regarded as inefficient in use of classroom space, but by arranging sessions on alternate days, five 4-credit courses can be accommodated in four classrooms. It is also possible to use periods of length greater than the usual 50 minutes and have only two or three class meetings.

probable that they would not be counted as satisfying the major requirements of the departments. The presence of such electives would permit and encourage students to broaden the scope of their education without forcing them into unreasonable competition with students better grounded in the area.

16. Departmental credit offerings should not exceed 40 semester credit hours (excluding the offerings suggested in 11 and 15).

17. At least 18 hours of the departmental major of 30–40 hours should be a common requirement for all majors in the department.

18. One or more courses in each department should be designated as independent study, thereby permitting emphasis or specialization appropriate for individuals or small groups of students. Many of the advanced courses now listed in departments could be dropped and considered as one of the possible areas of independent study.

19. The maximum number of credits from any single department acceptable for a degree should be 40.

20. Every departmental major statement should include delineation of areas appropriate for supporting study, not so much in terms of specific courses as in terms of blocks of relevant knowledge, abilities, and skills.

21. The objectives or levels of competency required for enrollment in and for credit in each course should be defined in sufficiently clear terms so that students may be properly placed and/or granted full credit for achievement, however attained.

Principles for concentration other than departmental majors

22. Some central purpose, unifying or integrative element should be indentifiable.

23. Some sequential characteristics should be present, insuring that depth rather than superficial contact with a series of related disciplines is achieved.

24. An identifiable core of organized knowledge and principles should be included.

25. The total credit hours required in the concentration should not exceed 48.

26. Acceptable concentrations need not be restricted to those listed in the university catalog; indeed, the attempt to list every acceptable concentration may be unwise, for it tends to encourage

choice of a listed pattern rather than the planning of one suited to the student's needs and interests.

Principles for the planning of students' programs

27. A statement of the purposes of each major and a justification for all the requirements and their sequence should be available to advisers and to prospective majors.

28. Student programs should be planned to maintain as much flexibility in vocational choice by the student as is consistent with preparation for activity in his present choice of vocation. This can be accomplished by emphasizing liberal and general professional study rather than specialized work, and by organizing distinctive curriculums which prepare the student for several related jobs rather than for particular specialties.

29. Both liberal and technical or professional work, on one hand, and breadth and depth, on the other, should be pursued throughout the entire program.

30. Early in the college career of each student, his entire college program should be tentatively mapped out by the student and his adviser. This plan should include some attention to all relevant experiences—not solely to required course work. The existence of a plan is important to give direction to the student; it should, however, be subject to change if the student changes his goals.

31. Acceleration by year-round attendance or by comprehensive examinations should be considered. This has implications both for efficient use of space and for wise use of the student's time.

32. Wherever possible, students should be encouraged and assisted to engage in work or service related to their major or specialized study. Experience in assisting a professor by checking freshman papers would encourage review and increased understanding; it might also interest some students in college teaching. Other students might select experiences directly related to their vocational choice.

33. Students should be encouraged to use their electives to explore unknown or unfamiliar areas.

34. Any full-time student should, upon authorization by his adviser, be permitted to visit any class (if space is available) and be permitted to take an examination for credit thereafter.

35. Each student should be encouraged (when it is appropriate)

to take a course offered by his adviser. Ultimately he should have an adviser in his field of interest.

36. The instructional methods and requirements of individual courses should be known to students and advisers, so that the program planned for the student may include laboratory, writing, speaking, discussion, case method, and other learning experiences significant in attaining a broad liberal education.

37. All students should take at least one course which exposes them to points of view, values, and cultures very different from their own.

38. All students should enroll in the senior year in an integrative senior seminar. This seminar should be organized on either a university-wide or a college-wide basis. Limited to groups not more than 25 students, the seminar should encourage them to review the summary implications of their university studies and experiences and the relationships of their past university activities to the role that they will shortly assume in society.

Faculty advisers would be expected to interpret these principles and to insist on the development of progress in conformity with them. Student programs should occasionally be reviewed to ascertain whether the spirit of these principles is being carefully followed.

Implications of the Principles

Since the principles which have just been presented have been derived out of a detailed analysis of problems and difficulties in existing undergraduate curriculums, the rationale for and implications of most of the principles are reasonably apparent. General principles 1–6 simply make explicit the model earlier presented, and provide for appropriate relationship and interaction of breadth and depth or specialization, whether for a major in the arts and sciences or for a vocationally-oriented undergraduate program. Principles 7 and 8 suggest criteria for planning or for the inclusion or elimination of curriculums and courses at the undergraduate level.

Principles 9–21 describe and restrict the nature of departmental offerings. Although these principles apply most obviously to the disciplines included in the arts and sciences, they apply also to vocational offerings if sub-specialties are defined through a departmental organization. Perhaps the most radical implication of these principles is found in the limitation on courses and hours. Yet there is more flexibility permitted than at first is apparent. The following pattern suggests how a departmental program consistent with these principles might look:

Department of History

Freshman Year	History 101	4 credits	Required
	History 102	4 credits	Sequence
			for
Sophomore Year	History 203	4 credits	History
	History 204	4 credits	Majors
Junior Year	History 305	4 credits	
	History 306	4 credits	
	History 307	4 credits	
Senior Year	History 408	4 credits	
	History 409	4 credits	
	History 410	3 credits	
	History 411	2 credits	
	(Independent Study, may be repeated)		

*Electives for Non-Majors **

History 350 3 credits
History 360 3 credits

* History 101, 102 prerequisites

The first-year courses would be so planned as to be equally attractive for majors and as breadth offerings for general education purposes. The first five courses would be prerequisites to all other courses in the major sequence. In addition, and still consistent with these principles, a few courses for non-majors might be offered. Also, a few special courses might be required for students in other curriculums when an adequate rationale for such a course is presented by the faculty controlling these curriculums. Special interests of individual majors could be supplied through judicious use of independent study. Furthermore, the student with such an experience would be much better prepared to continue reading history independently, if his interest continues after college. History, of course, has been selected only as an example; the same pattern could be readily applied to other disciplines.

In the large university, the tendency of each department to hire specialists in every sub-specialty of the discipline, and the desire of these specialists to teach in their particular area of interest, will make such restriction difficult to establish. In the small university and the liberal arts college, the more limited range of special competencies should dictate such restriction, for the offering of a wide range of courses by a faculty of limited range of competency is evidently not good educational practice. In either case, the tendency of any one department to extend unduly its range of offerings results inevitably in increased costs or the imposition of an unreasonable load on the faculty.

Administrative and Budgeting Procedures

The budget of a college or university must both reflect and support its educational purposes and programs. Thus the budgeting process must rely on evidence which reveals how resources—both human and financial—are being utilized and with what effect. The utilization of resources is revealed in some measure by data on faculty load, departmental credit-hour load, and unit costs. The quality of a program as revealed in the achievement of students or in completed research is not so easily appraised; dependence on subjective appraisal is inevitable. It is apparent, therefore, that budgetary decisions cannot be made solely on the basis of statistics on load and costs. Some principles regarding instructional load and productivity, amount of time spent in research, advising, and other activities would be desirable. Such principles must make allowances for inherent differences in the instructional requirements in various disciplines. Hence, acceptable and equitable principles are difficult to derive, and are not usually made explicit.

Two points that pertain especially to the curriculum and instructional organization should be taken into account. The first point is that a department which offers an unduly large number of courses relative to its enrollment necessarily ends up with small classes and expensive instruction. Furthermore, the use of occasional large lectures, or of a variety of learning resources, is effectively eliminated. Unless the nature of the discipline requires small classes, such a department utilizes an unfair proportion of the budget. Budgetary curtailment may be the most effective means of forcing curriculum reform.

The second point is that a department has no incentive for investigating new and more economical instructional patterns if the end result is that its savings go to support uneconomical expansion in other departments. Such savings must result in increased salaries or in other advantages to those who effect them.

Interpretation of the Program
to Students, Parents, and the General Public

The educational program resulting from the stated curriculum principles and enforced by budgetary policy would require extensive interpretation and "selling." Faculties would have to accept the program as advantageous to themselves in income and in personal satisfaction, and they would also have to agree that such a relatively restricted and more highly structured program would provide better education. If faculties are not receptive and even enthusiastic, there will be some difficulty in persuading students—and especially their parents—that curriculums providing somewhat less specialization and a narrower range of choice could possibly be as good as the more specifically vocationally related curriculums and courses available elsewhere. If, however, the curriculum is enthusiastically received and interpreted by the faculty and administration, it may be predicted that there will be no difficulty in attracting students and perhaps even a better and more highly motivated group. Colleges which choose to be unique in significant respects which relate to providing good education need have no qualms as to clientele. The difficulty with too many colleges, despite their emphasis on individuality and uniqueness, is that few administrators and faculties have the courage to be different.

As to the reaction of the general public, it may be stated with assurance that any college or university which, in times of increasing numbers and costs, finds more effective and efficient ways of providing higher education, will reap a harvest of publicity and applause which will encourage others to follow that model.

Summary

In this chapter, the attempt has been to develop a statement of principles governing the development of undergraduate curriculums. These principles are directed (1) to minimizing the distinction between liberal and vocational programs by principles which apply equally to both; (2) to restricting markedly the range of courses offered at the undergraduate level, on the grounds that better and more economical education can thereby be provided; (3)to encouraging students and advisers to plan more carefully the college period as a unitary educational experience; and (4) to suggesting administrative and budgetary procedures which will reinforce the curricular principles.

Finally, confidence has been expressed that such an approach to curricular planning can be interpreted to students and to the general public, so that an institution following such a pattern need not fear a loss of popularity or prestige. The major problem is likely to be that of attaining faculty acceptance and enthusiasm, for too few of the faculty members have an adequate perception of the total undergraduate experience.

CHAPTER VI

The Education of College
and University Professors

Oliver C. Carmichael,[1] in his book on graduate education, re-
marks as follows:

> This much is certain: the Ph.D. degree is no guarantee that its
> holder is qualified to give instruction in the liberal arts college. The
> nature of research performed even in the basic subjcts is often
> unrelated to liberal education and, as such, is not satisfactory prep-
> aration for college teaching. Despite the fact that this is generally
> recognized as true, the Ph.D. is still sought after since there is no
> other program designed to fill the needs of the prospective teacher.

Carmichael's statement is phrased specifically in reference to the
liberal arts college, but it is just as applicable to the university or
to any of the professional or technical schools within the university.

It is true that the research traditionally required as a part of the
Ph.D. candidate's training in the university has more specific
relevance to the role that he is expected to perform. Research is a
major function of a university, and the research productivity of a
university professor is more likely than any other factor to determine
his status in the university. For those professors whose sole responsibility is in the area of research or some combination of
research and graduate level teaching, it might seem that criticism
of the Ph.D. degree, because of its irrelevance to or inattention to
preparation for teaching, is misplaced. Even for college teaching,
the importance of a depth of knowledge in a specific field is un-
questionable. The research completed for the Ph.D. degree may
also have some relevance to teaching, if it provides some grasp of
the methodology of the field. Yet it remains evident that the majority
of those receiving the Ph.D. degree have given no systematic
attention to their role as college teachers.

---

[1] Oliver C. Carmichael, *Graduate Education: A Critique and Program* (New
York: Harper & Row, Publishers, 1961).

There are exceptions to this. Special degrees such as Doctor of Social Science, Doctor of Humanities, and the like have been developed in a few institutions to provide specific preparation for teaching, and especially for teaching in broad interdisciplinary areas suggested by the terms used. On the whole, however, these degrees are viewed as second-class degrees, and there is no pronounced trend toward their further development. A few individual departments and graduate schools make definite attempts to insure that those Ph.D. prospects interested in college teaching take some courses in the area of higher education or engage in some teaching under supervision. These efforts are commendatory but again they do not represent a significant trend in graduate study.

It is not likely that the majority of graduate faculty members would readily accept any education requirements such as have become customary in the preparation of teachers for elementary and secondary schools. First, there exists the blithe assumption that a person who really knows a field is perforce a good teacher. The assumption is readily refuted by the many examples of recognized scholars who are painfully disorganized and incoherent in the classroom. Knowledge is necessary but not sufficient.

The second basis for the rejection is the prevalent feeling that education courses are generally of low caliber. There is certainly some experience to support this point of view, and not very much in the way of evidence to demonstrate that the mastery of education courses has any more relevance to the preparation of teachers than has the mastery of the content provided by the traditional academic departments.

A third factor is that more and more Ph.D.'s are being hired by industry, government, and other fields. Indeed, in some of the science areas, the larger percentage of the students take industrial or governmental positions. It therefore appears unreasonable to require of every student one or more courses that might give him some background in college teaching. It is reasonable, however, to expect that the university provide some relevant set of experiences for those interested in college teaching. These experiences should include some knowledge of the development of American higher education, some awareness of its major current problems, some insight into the nature of the learning process, and some directed experience in the planning and teaching of undergraduate courses.

The Need for an Understanding
of the Essential Nature of Higher Education

Every prospective college faculty member should have some understanding of the nature of American higher education to foster more insight and understanding as a classroom teacher and to become a more intelligent participant in the decision-making role in faculty and committee meetings.

Every prospective college faculty member should also attain some understanding of the organization and administration of a college. The problems inherent in admission, counseling, residence halls, fund raising, budgetary allocation, and institutional self-study are much more complex than the average faculty member realizes. Much of the grumbling about "administration" and the suspicion of administrative policies could be alleviated if the prospective college teacher were to examine some of these matters on a broader basis than his personal and departmental objectives readily permit. One of the major shortcomings of faculty members is their inability to relate personal and departmental interests to the needs of the institution as a whole.

The Need for Attention to Instruction
and the Learning Process

The new Ph.D. seldom has any conception of the nature of the learning process and probably has not had his attention directed to the fact that there are many different ways of carrying on instruction. Experience in handling a graduate seminar on instructional problems for doctoral candidates demonstrates, for example, that many of them had never realized the distinction between a so-called discussion, in which all conversation is between the individual student and the teacher, and true discussion in which students converse with each other. The consideration of some of the different possible methods of instruction, of the relationships between these and objectives and various other factors in the planning of an instructional program, and possibly the experience of trying to use one or more of these methods, opens up whole new vistas of teaching to many doctoral candidates. It is not possible to talk intelligently about instruction without considering the nature of the learning process, and examining the relatively few known principles that operate. This, in turn, readily leads into some consideration of the obligations and functions of a teacher, and the possible realization that the selection of a textbook or the presentation of a lecture or a series of lectures hardly fulfills these obligations and functions.

Exciting new developments in the use of a wide variety of learning resources are imminent. Audio-visual aids have long been available on most university and college campuses, but they have been ineffectively used because they have been little understood by the college professor, and hence have received incidental use rather than being incorporated into the systematic planning of a program. Closed circuit television opens up the possibility of bringing many of these audio-visual aids into the classroom in a much more effective and efficient way than has been possible in the past. Programmed learning poses the possibility of placing much more emphasis on student activity, releasing the teachers from many of the chores for which they have been previously responsible. It is evident that any effective learning program requires concentrated effort by one or more teachers with insight and full awareness of the technical resources available. These teachers must be reasonably sophisticated as to the nature of learning, in addition to being well-versed in their subject matter field. This is not to suggest that the Ph.D. program should be designed to make each teacher an effective programmer. Surely, however, it is not unreasonable to maintain that every prospective college teacher should be brought in contact with the several ideas and possibilities which have been suggested with regard to instruction, curriculum planning, and the nature of learning.

The Necessity of In-Service Training of College Faculty Members

There is, however, no assurance that any large proportion of the graduate students will take advantage of such experiences. Even if it were assumed that they did, the fact remains that a large proportion of college teachers for some time to come will be those who are already employed in colleges and universities. Every institution, therefore, should plan a program of in-service training.

The possibilities include preparation of digests of some of the articles or books on instructional developments; maintenance of special faculty book shelves in the library; and provision of funds for providing each department a number of books, volumes, or articles dealing with the historical aspects of American higher education, its continuing problems, studies of instruction, accounts of developments in the use of new technological learning resources, and the like. A lecture series bringing to the campus authorities in these fields can be used to arouse interest. Grants which make it possible for individual faculty members to explore instructional problems or to visit other institutions where such projects are under way can be very effective. Recognition of those individuals who evidence interest in such matters also makes a real impact in focusing faculty attention on the nature of the problems faced in planning undergraduate curriculums.

The induction of new faculty members should include some seminar programs involving presentation and discussion of some of the essential ideas suggested earlier in this chapter and monograph. Some experience in planning and carrying through such sessions suggests that the novice faculty member is commonly highly appreciative of such a series and equally appreciative of the possibility that resources exist in the institution from which he can get continuing assistance. Experience also suggests that the greatest hazard to the success of such ventures is likely to be found among the senior professors or even the department heads who view such institutionally planned sessions as somehow a reflection on their own capability or as an interference with their own prerogatives. To avoid this reaction, their cooperation should be sought in every way possible. A further justification for the in-service training program of new faculty members is found in the existence of unique qualities in the program and philosophy of any particular institution. Although this uniqueness is sometimes overrated, it remains true that on any campus in which extensive curricular planning has already been carried on, new staff members do not readily assimilate the rationale for it, and even older ones need to be reminded, from time to time, of the underlying principles.

Reference has also been made to the rapid development of technological learning resources. It may be expected in the future that a wide range of films, videotapes, slides, programmed textbooks, live television production, and other materials will become available. The role of faculty members may change considerably, and there may be much more use of technical aids, much more insistence that the students be responsible for phases of their own learning, much more attention to relating residence halls and instructional programs, and a greater attempt to develop a total environment conducive to learning. This will require that each professor reconsider his role and enter into the planning of his course in a new manner which involves determining the best combination of all the available resources and possible experiences to achieve the objectives of his particular program. Clearly, also, such planning will require more thoughtful relating of single courses and curriculums to other courses and curriculums. It is altogether likely that such planning will require a team approach, in which one or more professors and a number of learning resources specialists and evaluators combine with a number of technicians to develop a complete program. The realization of such a possibility will require the development of a research and service center on a campus from which faculty members can get the specialized assistance that they need for such planning. It will also require a continuing in-service training program designed to acquaint college faculty members with what the possibilities are and to encourage them to overcome their natural reluctance or antipathy to change.

The Role of the Curriculum

It is no longer possible for any individual to come into meaningful contact with all the ideas presently subsumed under the phrase "liberal arts." It is equally true that education for any profession can no longer be defined in terms of the completion of some prescribed courses. The body of basic knowledge required in a profession is continually increasing, and the number of specific items of knowledge, skills, and abilities required for practicing the profession is also increasing. Education, then, must emphasize the development of a series of experiences which will develop in the individual both the desire and the ability to continue his own education.

In this view, the curriculum can no longer be regarded as a fixed set of courses. It must be regarded, rather, as defined by a set of principles which constitute a means of structuring the association of the teacher and the student to the end of educating the student. Neither in objectives nor in content are liberal and vocational education antithetical or even independent. Any vocation worthy of attention in a college or university must employ a body of substantive knowledge derived from what have been called the liberal arts. Any profession worthy of attention in a college or university likewise requires for performance the qualities associated with a liberal mind. By clarifying the nature of these qualities through the phrasing of objectives which specify the desired changes in behavior, by making these objectives explicit to students, and by developing a rich and varied set of learning experiences relevant to the accomplishment of these objectives, all undergraduate programs can turn out graduates who have the capability of continuing their learning.

Bibliography

Berelson, Bernard, *Graduate Education in the United States*. New York: McGraw-Hill Book Co., Inc., 1960.

Blauch, Lloyd E., ed., *Education for the Professions*. Washington, D.C.: Government Printing Office, 1955.

Boardman, Eugene P., ed., *Asian Studies in Liberal Education*. Association of American Colleges, 1959.

Boehm, Werner W., *The Social Work Curriculum Study*, 13 vols. New York: Council on Social Work Education, 1959.

Bonthius, Robert H., *et al.*, *Independent Study Programs in the United States*. New York: Columbia University, 1957.

Butts, R. Freeman, *The College Charts Its Course*. New York: McGraw-Hill Book Co., Inc., 1939.

Carmichael, Oliver C., *Graduate Education: A Critique and a Program*. New York: Harper & Row, Publishers, 1961.

Dressel, Paul L., *Liberal Education and Journalism*. New York: Institute of Higher Education, Bureau of Publications, Teachers College, Columbia University, 1960.

Dressel, Paul L., and Lewis B. Mayhew, *General Education: Explorations in Evaluation*. Washington, D.C.: American Council on Education, 1954.

Dressel, Paul L., Lewis B. Mayhew, and Earl J. McGrath, *The Liberal Arts as Viewed by Faculty Members in Professional Schools*. New York: Institute of Higher Education, Bureau of Publications, Teachers College, Columbia University, 1959.

Eddy, Edward D., *Colleges for Our Land and Time*. New York: Harper & Row, Publishers, 1957.

General Education in Engineering, American Society for Engineering Education, 1956.

Gordon, Robert A., and James E. Howell, *Higher Education for Business*. New York: Columbia University Press, 1959.

Hofstadter, Richard, and C. DeWitt Hardy, *The Development and Scope of Higher Education in the United States*. New York: Columbia University, 1952.

Holstein, Edwin J., and Earl J. McGrath, *Liberal Education and Engineering*. New York: Institute of Higher Education, Bureau of Publications, Teachers College, Columbia University, 1960.

Hong, Howard, ed., *Integration in the Christian Liberal Arts College*. Northfield, Minn.: St. Olaf College Press, 1956.

101

Mayhew, Lewis B., ed., *General Education: An Account and Appraisal.* New York: Harper & Row, Publishers, 1960.

McConnell, T. R., *A General Pattern for American Public Higher Education.* New York: McGraw-Hill Book Co., Inc., 1962.

McGlothlin, William J., *Patterns of Professional Education.* New York: G. P. Putnam's Sons, 1960.

McGrath, Earl J., *The Graduate School and the Decline of Liberal Education.* New York: Institute of Higher Education, Bureau of Publications, Teachers College, Columbia University, 1959.

————, *Liberal Education in the Professions.* New York: Institute of Higher Education, Bureau of Publications, Teachers College, Columbia University, 1959.

————, *Memo to a College Faculty Member.* New York: Institute of Higher Education, Bureau of Publications, Teachers College, Columbia University, 1961.

McGrath, Earl J., and Charles H. Russell, *Are Liberal Arts Colleges Becoming Professional Schools?* New York: Institute of Higher Education, Bureau of Publications, Teachers College, Columbia University, 1958.

National Society for the Study of Education, *The Integration of Educational Experiences,* Fifty-Seventh Yearbook, Part III. Chicago: University of Chicago Press, 1958.

Newcomer, James, Kevin P. Bunnell, and Earl J. McGrath, *Liberal Education and Pharmacy.* New York: Institute of Higher Education, Bureau of Publications, Teachers College, Columbia University, 1960.

Pierson, Frank C., *et al., The Education of American Businessmen,* The Carnegie Series in American Education. New York: McGraw-Hill Book Co., Inc., 1959.

Pryor, Joseph E., *A Study of Senior College Curricula.* University of Chicago, 1949–50.

Rudy, Willis, *The Evolving Liberal Arts Curriculum: A Historical Review of Basic Themes.* New York: Institute of Higher Education, Bureau of Publications, Teachers College, Columbia University, 1960.

Russell, Charles H., *Liberal Education and Nursing.* New York: Institute of Higher Education, Bureau of Publications, Teachers College, Columbia University, 1959.

Schmidt, George P., *The Liberal Arts Colleges—A Chapter in American History.* New Brunswick, N.J.: Rutgers University, 1957.

Smith, Huston, *Purposes of Higher Education.* New York: Harper & Row, Publishers, 1955.

Smith, Leo F., and Lawrence Lipsett, *The Technical Institute.* New York: McGraw-Hill Book Co., Inc., 1956.

Snow, Louis S., *The College Curriculum in the United States.* New York: Teachers College, Columbia University, 1907.

Stewart, Blair, *Liberal Arts and Medical Education.* Oberlin, Ohio: Oberlin College, 1957.

Thomas, Russell, *The Search for a Common Learning: General Education 1800–1960*. New York: McGraw-Hill Book Co., Inc., 1962.

Wilson, James W., and Edward H. Lyons, *Work-Study College Programs, Appraisal and Report of the Study of Cooperative Education*. New York: Harper & Row, Publishers, 1961.

Index

Index

A

Academic freedom, 62
Accreditation, 53
  in undergraduate specialties, 14-15
Advising, 63, 71
Agricultural and mechanical colleges, 10
Antioch College, 13, 54
Area-study concept, 15-16
  relation to military enterprise, 15
Assessment of programs, 52-53
Assumptions about education, 72-74

B

Bachelor of Science degree, 11
Bennington College, 13
Black Mountain College, 13
Breadth, 77
  in curriculum, 33-34
  and sequence, 77
  in undergraduate program, 76-77
Budget and administration, 89
  dependence on appraisal, 89

C

California, University of, 7
Chicago, University of, 13
Clark University, 8
College catalogs, emphasis on vocationalism in, 42
Colleges, 75
  of commerce, 9
  departments in, 75-76
  early American, 1
  of engineering, 65-66
  state support of, 2
  in a university, 75-76
College teachers, 63, 64, 93-99
  in-service training of, 96
  professional preparation, 64
  and seminars, 97
Composition requirement, 45
Comprehensive examinations, 44, 86
Continuity in curriculum, 31
Cornell University, 5
Courses, 67
  duplication of, 62
  emphasis in, 67

Courses (*Cont.*)
  interdisciplinary, 67
  planning of, 67-68
  proliferation of, 17, 48, 55
Course loads, 89
  and budget, 89
  and depth, 78-79
  planning by students, 86-87
  and student population, 89
Course requirements, 66-67, 80-81
  in college curriculums, 56
  in philosophy, 46
  in technical and professional curriculums, 80-82
  in undergraduate programs, 66-67
  variations in, 56
Credit requirements, 82-87
  in arts and sciences, 81-82
  in college curriculums, 56
  in freshman composition, 45
  in technical and professional curriculums, 81-82
Curriculum, classical, 2
Curriculum development, 25-26, 82-87
  electives in, 83-84
  experiments in, 13
  history since 1900, 12-17
  principles of, 82-91
Curriculum model, 81, 90
  credit requirements, 81
  need for faculty acceptance of, 91
  in occupational and vocational curriculums, 38-40
  in preparation for graduate study, 37
  in pre-professional undergraduate program, 37

D

Dartmouth College, 11, 13
Departmentalization, 55-56, 61-62
  and comprehensive examinations, 44
  in universities, 46-50
Departments, 75-76
  in colleges, 75-76
  of vocational colleges, 55
Depth, 78-79
  in curriculum, 32-33, 71
  and sequence, 77
  in undergraduate program, 76
Duplication in courses, 62